Echoes of the Ancient World
Series editor Werner Forman

THE WAY OF THE SAMURAI

The summer grasses
For many brave warriors
The aftermath of dreams
Bashō

THE WAY OF THE SAMURAI

Richard Storry
Photographs by Werner Forman

GALLEY PRESS
A Division of W. H. Smith Publishers Inc.
112 Madison Avenue
New York City 10016

For Terence

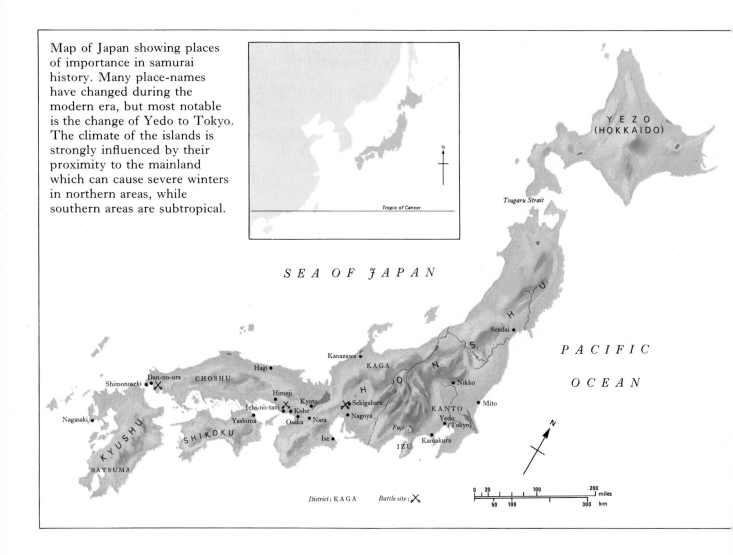

Map of Japan showing places of importance in samurai history. Many place-names have changed during the modern era, but most notable is the change of Yedo to Tokyo. The climate of the islands is strongly influenced by their proximity to the mainland which can cause severe winters in northern areas, while southern areas are subtropical.

© Orbis Publishing Limited, London 1978
Text © Richard Storry, 1978

Published by Galley Press
An imprint of W H Smith Publishers Inc., 112 Madison Avenue, New York, New York 10016

ISBN 0-8317-7675-7

Printed in Singapore by Toppan Printing Company
1 2 3 4 5 6 7 8 9

Endpapers: Detail from a screen depicting the siege of Osaka Castle. Page 1: Portrait of Minamoto Yoshitomo. Pages 2-3: Himeji Castle

Author's note: Japanese usage has normally been followed in the case of individual names; that is to say, the family name is followed by the personal name – for example in Tokugawa Ieyasu, Tokugawa is the family name. In one or two modern cases, however, such as Inazō Nitobe and Kenzō Tange, the Western style has been adopted.

CONTENTS

THE SILENT WARRIOR

The image of the samurai

In these declining years of the twentieth century no political or social concept is less fashionable than that of a hereditary martial governing class. For most people, indeed, the very idea of a *corps d'élite* suggests high-handed and insensitive arrogance. Historical models abound: Norman barons, Spanish hidalgos, Prussian officers. In their company must be included the *bushi*, or warrior class of Japan, commonly known as the samurai. But there have often been serious misconceptions concerning the history, character, beliefs and functions of the samurai, especially in societies remote from the Japanese. These distorted views have been nourished by strong emotions, and have oscillated between the two extremes of admiration and abhorrence.

Within living memory, Togo's annihilation of the Tsar's fleet and Nogi's capture of Port Arthur provoked a world-wide, compelling curiosity about the little known country whose soldiers and sailors had displayed both chivalry and courage in their war against the Russians. It was to be expected that the people of England, linked by a treaty of alliance with the Japanese, would welcome the outcome of the struggle and would accord Japan the title 'The Britain of the Far East'. It was natural, too, that the populations of Asia from the Yellow Sea to the Persian Gulf should have felt a deep satisfaction at the proof that the white race could no longer boast its invincible military power with such complete assurance. The Americans were greatly stirred by Japan's victory; the Tsarist government for many reasons, not least its spasmodic ill-treatment of Russian and Polish Jews, had long received a bad press throughout the United States. Thus, in Europe, Asia and America the

7

question raised in genial amazement was 'What is the secret of Japan's success?'

The most impressive answer to this question seemed to come from a little book called *Bushidō, The Soul of Japan*, written by a professor of Tokyo Imperial University, Dr Inazō Nitobe. This work, now almost completely forgotten, was in its day a bestseller in Britain and America. First published in 1900, it ran to no less than 17 editions during the next 12 years. Dr Nitobe received his higher education in the United States, where he joined the Quakers. After returning to Japan he won a well-earned reputation as a Christian teacher and writer, but one who by no means turned his back on the traditional religions and ethics of Japan. For example, in one of his books, entitled *Ichi-nichi ichi-gen (A Word a Day)*, he commended precepts from Buddhism, Confucianism and ancient Japanese poetry, as well as from the Bible.

In his preface to *Bushidō, The Soul of Japan* Nitobe explains that the idea of writing the book in English for foreign readers came to him when a Belgian visitor asked him what kind of religious instruction he had been given in his early school-days. Nitobe then realized that he had received no religious education as such, yet he had been brought up in a strongly ethical environment. During the enforced idleness of a long illness, reflecting on the nature and significance of that early environment, Nitobe wrote his book. The contents, he tells us, 'consist mainly of what I was taught and told in my youthful days, when feudalism was still in force'. He declares that 'without understanding feudalism and *bushidō*, the moral ideas of present Japan are a sealed volume'. It was the promise implicit in these words that attracted readers across the globe, especially in the years just after the Russo-Japanese War.

They were not disappointed. An American historian of medieval Japan, H. Paul Varley, has made the somewhat caustic observation that the style and content of Nitobe's book 'can today most charitably be called quaint'.[1] This may be so; Nitobe was nevertheless highly successful in popularizing certain fundamental elements of Japanese thought and behaviour of which Europeans and Americans had hitherto been largely ignorant. Until his book appeared, the English-speaking world had formed its ideas on Japan mainly through the intimations picked up from travellers' tales and Gilbert and Sullivan's *Mikado* (the style and content of which were designedly 'quaint').

Bushidō, The Soul of Japan exalts the traditions, standards and style of the samurai. Nitobe painted a glossy, idealized picture, one that was bound to appeal to the romantic imagination of his readers. His samurai are knights, *sans peur et sans reproche*. Having absorbed this, the Edwardian reader came to the kernel of Nitobe's message: *bushidō*, the ethical code of the samurai, was still alive. No longer confined to the old warrior class, it had spread its bracing influence throughout Japanese society. This explained the heroism and self-sacrifice shown on the battlefield, and the stoicism with which families saw their menfolk off to war. Furthermore, Nitobe's readers would gain the strong impression that the individual Japanese samurai of old was very much the same kind of person, with only a few superficial differences, chiefly sartorial, as a Highland laird or a Southern gentleman.

This favourable view of their traditional and still extremely influential ruling class was one that most Japanese could scarcely wish to discourage. But in so far as it was unreal it was potentially dangerous. Expectations were aroused that made subsequent disillusionment all the more savage. Less than 30 years after the Russo-Japanese War, for reasons we need not go into here, Japan, land of heroes, had been replaced by Japan, the imperialist capitalist parvenu. Worse was to follow. The Pacific War, its immediate aftermath, and the release of prisoners-of-war and internees from the camps in South-East Asia, seemed to make Nitobe's message at best a cruel farce. In the immediate post-war years the very word *bushidō* continued to evoke repulsive memories. Nor were these restricted to

The precise origins of the Japanese people remain a mystery, although Chinese records throw some light on Japanese culture in the early centuries AD.
Below: This terra-cotta figure of a kneeling man is one of many such objects discovered grouped around tombs and dating from the fourth to seventh centuries AD. Called haniwa, *they were originally simply cylinders but in later times the tops were moulded into shapes representing houses, animals or human beings. This figure appears to be wearing a horned headdress which suggests a link with primitive shamanism known to have been practised in Japan.*
Right: Two rocks at Futamigaura in Ise Bay, said to have sheltered the deities Izanagi and Izanami, who were among the legendary creators of Japan. The Wedded Rocks, as they are called, are linked by a straw rope (shimenawa) of the kind to be found hung in front of most Shinto shrines. In January every year the shimenawa *is replaced at a special ceremony. The spectacle of the sun rising behind the Wedded Rocks has been cherished by the Japanese from the earliest times*

Japan's former enemies; a large and vocal proportion of the Japanese people seemed almost equally hostile to the samurai tradition. Those who tried to defend it could only plead that its modern heirs had sullied a fine heritage by their brutality and folly.

By 1958 Japan had become a close ally of America and *The Seven Samurai* had been applauded in film theatres from London to Los Angeles, but in that year the book that might be called the antithesis of Nitobe was published, *The Knights of Bushidō* by Lord Russell of Liverpool. In this account of wartime atrocities the samurai spirit was depicted as treacherous and sadistic, and the guilty men were arraigned as the Nazis of the Far East. Lord Russell's book never attained the success enjoyed by Nitobe's, but its impact was considerable for a time. It revived, particularly on the European side of the Atlantic, the antipathy felt towards the Japanese Imperial forces and, by extension, towards everything associated with the samurai tradition.

By the 1970s we have a different image located somewhere between the extremes embodied in these two books, but the picture is still not clear. The samurai, after all, is a figure from the past who, it seems, fits in hardly at all with the modern Japanese scene. So how do we visualize him? He is, of course, the top-knotted swordsman, ready to take on single-handed a dozen foes. He is the warrior on the print or folding screen, in a carapace of dark armour with a winged helmet and grimacing mask. We see him fighting to the last as the castle falls in flames, or kneeling placidly on the immaculate *tatami,* the dirk poised to enter the left side of the belly. Perceived today through Western eyes he appears totally exotic, more remote from us than any paladin of the age of European chivalry, stranger than a mandarin of imperial China or shaman of the Tartar steppe.

Yet three bizarre events of the 1970s serve to remind us that the ghost of the samurai has not been laid. In November 1970, Japan's best known novelist committed *hara-kiri* in traditional *bushi* style. In March 1974, an Imperial Army lieutenant emerged from the jungles of Lubang in the Philippines after some 30 years of implacable defiance. In March 1976, a young actor deliberately crashed a light plane onto a suburban house in Tokyo, hoping thereby to kill not only himself but also the owner of the house whom he had come to hate and despise for alleged corruption. It was an operation carried out in conscious emulation of the wartime *tokkōtai,* the kamikaze pilots, who were themselves consciously emulating the heroism of the samurai. None of these three events, then, can be understood outside the context of the samurai code.

In the sacred woods of Ise stand the most important Shinto shrines, dedicated to the Sun Goddess and the Goddess of Cereals. They date from the third century AD, although they have been rebuilt every 20 years. Right: The characteristic roof of the Naikū, the Inner Shrine at Ise, with V-shaped wooden projections (chigi) and wooden cylinders across the ridge. The Naikū is said to have been built by an emperor who feared to keep the shrine to Amaterasu, the Sun Goddess and most powerful of the kami, *in his palace. Housed here, too, is part of the imperial regalia, emphasizing the crucial link between the emperor and Shinto.*
Far right: The ceremonial gateway, or torii, *to the outermost of the four courtyards surrounding the Ise shrines. The origins of these simple structures, characteristic of many Shinto shrines, are unknown*

Such episodes focus the mind on the blood and thunder aspect of the tradition, as indeed do the *chanbara eiga*—the samurai melodramas that are a staple fare of Japanese television and cinema screens. These stories constitute Japan's version of the 'Western', an analogy which can also work in reverse—the character played by Yul Brynner in *The Magnificent Seven* is essentially a samurai in a sombrero.

But do these modern images bring one any closer to reality? Who were the samurai? What were they really like? Can we make valid generalizations about a martial class that comprised perhaps five or six per cent of the population and yet dominated Japanese society for 700 years?

About the precise origins of the samurai, and indeed of the Japanese people as a whole, there is great obscurity. In remote antiquity, Japan may well have been colonized by waves of immigrants from the islands of the south-western Pacific as well as from the continent of Asia. No historical records appear to exist concerning such movements of people, but Japanese folklore—a potent mythology exalted in the 1930s to the status of a national faith—relates that the country was founded by certain deities of High Heaven, and that in due course the Sun Goddess sent her grandson to a mountain peak in Kyushu with instructions to rule the divinely created 'Central Land of Reed Plains'. His great-grandson, in

several years of fighting, advanced eastward along the shores of the Inland Sea to the Yamato region, south of modern Kyoto, and there established the first capital of Japan.

This shadowy figure was Jimmu Tennō, the first of the long line of emperors. He and his followers, the ancestors of the modern Japanese, evidently subdued by force of arms an existing indigenous race. Their victims were possibly the forebears of the Ainu, people of Caucasian stock who inhabited northern Honshu in historic times and who survive to this day in the island of Hokkaido, though in very small numbers.

Since the first emperor and his successors were revered as descendants of the Sun Goddess, and because the Japanese believed the mountains, plains, forests, streams and rocks of their country were of direct divine origin, the seeds were sown of two cults which together comprise *Shintō* and which were to exert a permanent influence on the psychology of the race. The first of these may be described as a special veneration for the sun. The second, closely related to the first, was an acutely sensitive awareness of nature—not only the changing seasons but also the trees, plants and soil that comprise the environment of mankind.

The Ise Shrines, some 70 miles (120 km) from Nagoya, symbolize these two cults. The Naikū (The Inner Shrine) is dedicated to the worship of Amaterasu—Omikami, the Sun Goddess. At the Geku (The Outer Shrine), four miles (6·5 km) away, veneration is paid to Toyouke-Omi-kami, the Goddess of Cereals. The striking feature of the Ise Shrines is their simplicity. They are plain wooden structures with steeply pitched thatched roofs. Yet, as Kenzō Tange, the architect, puts it: 'Plain to the point of artlessness, they nevertheless possess a highly refined style. Their origin has stamped on them an elementary vigour; they combine with this a timeless aesthetic discipline. Seldom is an architecture created in which the vital and aesthetic are as well balanced as here.'[2]

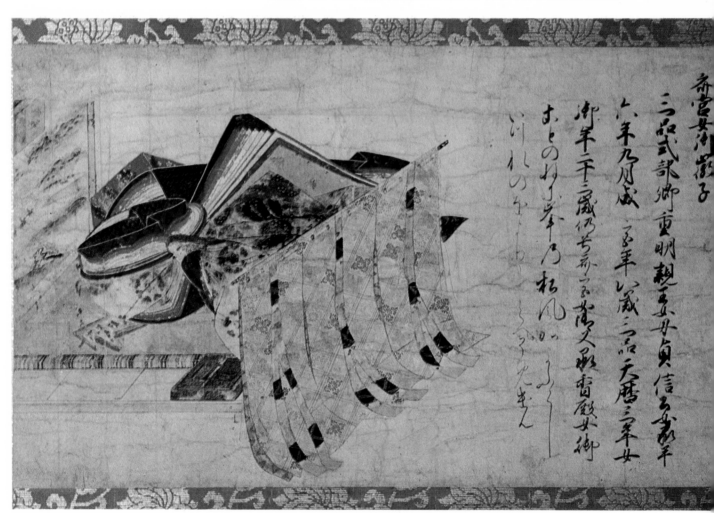

Japanese civilization during the Heian period was elegant, quietist and refined. Although the samurai brought about the destruction of Heian culture, they later idealized the period as a 'golden age'.

Above: Sculpture of the priest Hoshi from the end of the Heian period in the twelfth century. This priest was reputed to be the incarnation of a deity, and it is the face of the deity that is emerging so dramatically from that of the priest.

Left: A portrait from an emakimono, *or picture scroll, evocative of the splendours of Heian Kyoto in the early years of samurai power. The scroll, attributed to Fujiwara Nobuzane, shows portraits of 36 great poets and poetesses of the Heian age. This portrait is of Saigū no Nyōgo, the poetess, whose poem is inscribed on the scroll. 'The breeze rustles the leaves on the hillside and seems to mingle with the tone of the* koto. *On which string of the* koto, *I wonder, does the breeze begin to play?' (The* koto *is a type of horizontal harp)*

No real understanding of the Japanese is possible unless it takes account of their feeling for what is plain, unvarnished, simple. This may appear strange to those who have seen the ugliness and vulgarity that characterizes much of Japanese modern urbanized life. It is true, furthermore, that Japan's history can show us periods in which highly decorative arts flourished and gaudy excess was esteemed. But in every case, from the splendours of the Nara age in the eighth century AD to the metropolitan extravaganza of Tokyo in the 1970s the inspiration has come from abroad, whether from T'ang China or twentieth-century America. The truly indigenous instinct is invariably towards what is austere and, indeed, ascetic.

Related to this is the factor, of crucial importance in earlier years and still significant, of insularity. Until the age of the steamship the Japanese islands were by no means easily accessible, even from the Asian mainland. The Tsushima Straits, separating Japan from Korea, were sufficiently wide and meteorologically hazardous to protect the homogeneity of the Japanese since the legendary Jimmu Tennō's time.

Self-sufficient in their mountainous archipelago, convinced of their special providence under the shield of the Sun Goddess and countless other deities, or *kami* as they were known, animists in their attention to nature, plain and vigorous in their instincts, the Japanese possessed a hard core which no influences from outside—not even those as powerful and pervasive as Buddhist metaphysics and Confucian ethics—could eradicate or absorb. From such stock rose, in the eleventh century, the distinctive military class of the samurai.

The samurai class was not merely a durable oligarchy of Far Eastern protofascists, though such a label, however unhistorical from a severely pedantic point of view, should not be entirely dismissed. There is a sense, certainly, in which the samurai can be described as usurpers. Long before they could stake a claim for any share in governing the country, during the so-called Heian period, Japan displayed one of the most attractive and elegant metropolitan civilizations known to history. It survived for generations without suffering any great interference in governmental affairs at the hands of the samurai. In this regard China had set an example which Heian Japan was able to follow.

Once the samurai had become irresistible and permanent intruders in government, however, many of them over the years acquired the airs and graces of the court aristocracy whom they had eased out of all but nominal authority in the state administration. The process is one with which the historian is familiar. The barbarian in close contact with his betters acquires sooner or later something of their polish, if not the very finest attributes of their culture. The Goths and other tribes during the decadence and collapse of the Roman Empire display a close parallel. In the case of Japan the process was furthered by intermarriage between powerful warrior houses and the imperial family. Nevertheless, it was not considered fitting that a samurai should give himself wholly to the pursuit of scholarly or artistic excellence if this meant that his skill as a fighting man might be impaired. Progress in civility must be balanced by continued practice of the military arts. As a Japanese wartime slogan had it, *zeitaku wa teki da!*—'Luxury is the Enemy!'

The composition of the warrior class changed drastically during the years of civil war between the middle years of the fifteenth century and the end of the sixteenth. As one historian, G. B. Sansom, has pointed out: 'so far as concerns the personnel of her dominant classes, Japan was entirely refashioned by the year 1600'.[3] Despite all the changes, however, traditions remained. Those who in that turbulent age had risen from obscurity—foot-soldiers or peasants who became great captains—were eager to accept, genuinely or with lip-service, the code of morality and conduct peculiar to the samurai. Thus, before the seventeenth century, the samurai class was often infused with new blood. Even during the socially rigid days of the Tokugawa shogunate, from the early seventeenth century to the middle of the nineteenth, there was some movement into and out of the ranks of the samurai. But the traditions remained; the code endured. It was these which gave the samurai his high standing in his own eyes and in those of society as a whole.

A number of religious, philosophical, and aesthetic elements mingled to produce the psyche of the 'ideal' samurai. The duty of staunch loyalty to one's lord was a primordial imperative, essential in most tribal societies and not to be despised in those that claim to be more advanced. It was enhanced—was given, we might say, scriptural authority—by the force of Confucian doctrines. The samurai's attitude to death was also fundamental to his way of thought. Death was 'lighter than a feather', showing that the influence of Buddhism was profound. Buddhism, specifically Zen Buddhism, played a vital part in training the samurai to command both himself and the use of his weapons: sword, bow, spear, or musket. It was Zen that gave birth to the ritual of the tea ceremony, an inspiration before battle and a relaxation afterwards. As for *seppuku* (the formal name for the rite of *hara-kiri*), this was assuredly influenced by emanations from Shinto sources. At its best, the life-style of a samurai of the Tokugawa period (1603–1867) exemplified a form of art, austere and limited

The Japanese garden in all its beauty was a source of exquisite contemplative content.
Right: The 'sea of silver sand'. In this famous Zen garden of the Ginkaku-ji, Kyoto, the arrangement symbolizes the sea and mountains, with a simple mound which reflects the moonlight when viewed from the pavilion.
Below: The serene garden of the Saihō-ji is famous for its mosses, of which there are more than 100 species. It is traditionally associated with the powerful and astute priest Musō Kokushi (1235–1351). But although he rehabilitated the garden, it has an earlier history, and was originally conceived in the seventh century

but not ignoble. His predecessors in an earlier age, during the epic struggle of the Gempei War of the twelfth century, were perhaps more colourful, but they too could demonstrate, from time to time, qualities that pertain to the realm of art no less than the sphere of ethics.

When considering the psychological make-up and organizational structure of the samurai class it is natural to look for convincing historical parallels in other societies. The one that springs readily to mind is that of the European knight in the age of high-feudalism, for example during the time of the Angevin Empire. As far as we know, however, knight and samurai never met and probably had barely an inkling of each other's existence. But 400 years ago an encounter did take place between the samurai and members of a European *élite* modelled along the lines of a military caste; indeed, its founder had himself been a fighting man.

The Society of Jesus, 'the cavalry of the Church', was extremely successful for some decades following its arrival in south-western Japan. There is plenty of evidence to show that Jesuit fathers and Japanese samurai were in many instances drawn to each other by feelings of mutual respect. Francis Xavier's words of praise for the Japanese are well known: 'I do not think you will find their match among the pagan nations. They are very sociable, usually good and not malicious, and much concerned with their honour, which they prize above everything else . . . They have one characteristic which is not to be found in any part of Christendom: however poor a noble may be . . . they pay him as much honour as if he were rich . . . The people hold the gentry in great respect, and in their turn the nobles are proud to serve their lord, obeying his least command. And this, I fancy, is not due to any fear of punishment which the lord might inflict for disobedience, but rather on account of the loss of honour that they would suffer if they were to do otherwise.'[4]

It should be noted that Xavier refers to 'honour' no less than three times in this short passage. Despite a close affinity, this concept of honour is not the same as 'face'. Important as it is, face carries less weight than honour, and in feudal Japan those outside as well as those within the samurai order—merchants, for example, or craftsmen—could possess face, a quality that could be enhanced, saved, or lost. Honour, on the other hand, was something more, something extra, an addition to the moral cargo that every samurai was expected to carry. Anthropologists seem to agree that Japanese society was—and still is to a significant extent—a 'shame culture'. To this day it is usual, as it may always have been in the case of most households, for a Japanese mother to warn a child that eccentric behaviour will make it an object of ridicule. 'If you do that' she might say, 'people will laugh at you'. There is a world of

Samurai power reached its most ostentatious development in the Momoyama and Tokugawa periods under the dictator Toyotomi Hideyoshi and the first Tokugawa shogun, Ieyasu.

Left : An example of the elaborate style of decoration used in Hideyoshi's Fushimi Castle. Parts of the castle have now been incorporated into a Kyoto temple, but an atmosphere of lavish splendour remains linked to Hideyoshi's name in the popular imagination. The walls and screens were the work of artists of the Kanō school.

Above : The equipment of the samurai throughout the ages combined artistic excellence with practical utility, as can be seen in this beautiful tsuba, *or sword-guard, which displays a scene of a fox disguising itself as a woman*

difference between that and the more frequent parental injunction in the West: 'Don't mind if people laugh at you', where the implication is that one must follow one's own conscience and ignore what other people say.

This more Western attitude also existed to a small extent in Japan during the feudal age, however, and was to be found among some members of the warrior classes. In other words, samurai honour embraced the ideal of personal integrity and included, therefore, some notion of free will and even of the primacy of the individual. As we shall see, loyalty to one's lord did not call for dumb obedience in every conceivable situation, indeed true loyalty might demand respectful but serious protest, and in extreme cases remonstrance against a superior by *seppuku*.

There are also examples of gross disloyalty and bad faith among the samurai: *corruptio optimi pessima*—the corruption of the best is worst of all, as the sixteenth century Jesuits would have said. These missionaries, doubtless because they thought so highly of the warrior class among whom they lived and which provided the bulk of their early converts, did not hesitate to cite in their correspondence instances of samurai treachery, vengefulness and heartless brutality. While competence in the military arts and plain courage were taken for granted as two fundamental constituents in the character of every samurai, it would be a crude mistake, of course, to imagine that the samurai order did nothing else but fight or prepare for battle. It was, after all, for centuries the ruling class of Japan and was therefore heavily engaged in national and local administration at every level above that of the rural village. This administration was very much government for, as well as by, the samurai class. This did not necessarily mean that the common man found government invariably oppressive, but even at the best of times he had to tread warily. Modern Japanese is a 'respect language', gilded with honorifics and replete with circumlocutions. Fanciful though it may be, one cannot help feeling that this owes something to the need, in ages past, not to provoke the possibly uncertain temper of the warrior as he rode by the rice-fields. The long sword, lethal and beautiful, imposed outward deference. The short sword, symbol of suicide, commanded inner respect.

That this self-confident martial class would apply itself with a will to learning the military techniques of the West might have been foreseen. What is much more surprising is the thoroughness with which so many samurai threw themselves, during the last 30 years of the nineteenth century, into the manifold professions and commercial activities characteristic of Western society. It could hardly have been predicted at the beginning of the nineteenth century that the Japanese warrior, with his inherited contempt for the merchant and indeed for money as such, would ever think of becoming a banker, mill-owner, or general trader. Yet, as often as not, the samurai proved to be a more successful businessman than the commoner who belonged to the traditional merchant class. This suggests that there was an element of down-to-earth pragmatism in the character of many a samurai. The warrior was not unwilling to make money when the activity could be rationalized as a civic and, indeed, patriotic duty.

Finally, another phenomenon is worth noting. The leading figures in dissident, radical circles of the intelligentsia in the late nineteenth and early twentieth centuries were nearly all of samurai stock. If the Japanese ultra-nationalism of this century was nurtured by the samurai ethos, resolute, though unsuccessful, opposition to this trend by a small socialist minority was led by those who also belonged to those traditions.

The authentic nature of the samurai, therefore, was a good deal more complex and paradoxical than the conventional picture might imply. The pages that follow attempt to illustrate how and why this was so. They trace the main course of samurai activities through some seven centuries and more of Japanese history, pausing on the way in order to examine religious, aesthetic and ethical signposts in the story as, like an *emakimono*, or picture scroll of the Heian age, it unfolds before the reader.

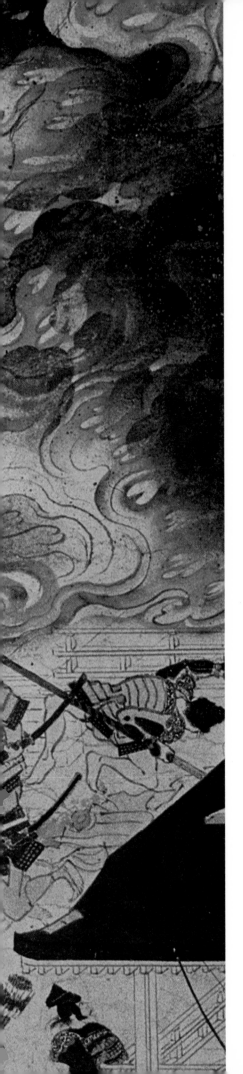

THE
SAMURAI
EMERGES

The making of a class

Kyoto, the historic capital of Japan, dates its foundation from the year AD 794. Known in those days as Heiankyō, it gave that name to one of the most elegant civilizations on record. Lettered, humane, and profoundly aesthetic, this was the refined and engaging world portrayed by the court lady, Murasaki Shikibu, in *Genji Monogatari (The Tale of Genji)*[1]. The elegance of Heian culture is suggested by the fact that (as one authority puts it) this civilization 'was, to a quite remarkable extent, based on aesthetic discrimination and, with the rarest of exceptions, every gentleman and lady was an amateur performer in one or more of the arts'.[2] Meticulous attention was paid to the formal, the ceremonious, the graceful in life and art. It was an aristocratic culture in the true sense, hostile to all that was crude, violent, and vulgar. The Heian court nobility was supremely concerned with style. Learning, speculative religion, questions of social morality, were held to be subsidiary to the more important values attached to excellence in poetry and calligraphy, to felicity in costume and demeanour.

In theory the imperial court at Kyoto, at the apex of government, administered the whole country. The government, following a pattern established in China, claimed the ownership of all land, while the tillers of the soil payed taxes in produce and labour services. In practice, however, there was also a network of tax-free estates, which at first had been confined to virgin land brought under cultivation. In course of time this

Left: The burning of the Sanjō Palace in Kyoto, from a picture scroll of the Heiji Insurrection, one of the first samurai battles

19

restriction became inoperative, and parcels of tax-free land were allotted to Buddhist temples, members of the imperial and other families in Kyoto, provincial governors or their deputies, and local worthies. In a mountainous and heavily forested country such as Japan territorial sentiment is always strong, and it was never easy for Kyoto to exercise effective control on areas distant from the capital. Moreover, as metropolitan culture flowered, the contrast between the civility of Kyoto and the rough conditions of provincial life became ever greater.

Appointment to a governorship far from the Heian court was often most unwelcome. Administrative service in, for example, the Kantō Plain (the region of modern Tokyo) some 300 miles (480 km) away, might mean permanent separation from the sophisticated attractions of the capital, for the journey was long and arduous. Once it was over, however, the Kyoto noble, much like the Victorian migrant to America or Australia, might feel inclined to make the best of things, settle, and eventually come to identify himself closely with 'the new country'. Sometimes successful efforts were made to avoid such exiles by securing agreement that the governorship would be exercised by a deputy. Nevertheless, rustication was a convenient method of placing members of the imperial family, as well as those of the related nobility, in useful employment and out of mischief.

The samurai class first emerged in frontier territory, so horses and equestrian prowess were of great importance to them. The best horses came from the Kantō region and from the mountainous areas of northern Japan.

Above and left: These magnificent representations of the warrior's horse are from a sixteenth-century painted screen. The samurai looked for spirit and liveliness in their mounts. In the stable the horse could be given some exercise by the use of a girth suspended from the roof of the stable. *Above left*: A scene from a seventeenth-century painted screen showing the traditional craftsmen at work. In this scene the rawhide workers are busy making saddles and leather equipment

Though the links with Kyoto always remained, provincial life, especially in the east and north-east, bred its own species. Quite early we come across references to the *Azuma-bito,* or 'men of the east'. This refers to a recognizable type, somewhat uncouth by Kyoto standards, but courageous and skilled in the use of bow, spear and sword. Such men extended the boundaries of settlement and cultivation, fighting the tribes now presumed to be ancestors to the modern Ainu. Heian Japan's frontier country could be called her 'Wild East', meaning the country north as well as east of the Fuji Lakes.

In that area—and in others where distance from Kyoto and personal ambition might point the way—provincial officials and their families acclimatized to their localities, and carved out for themselves semi-independent baronies. These were defended and at times enlarged by bands of warriors, *bushi-dan* as they were known. In origin these warbands appear to have been a family affair, their core consisting of a family chief, his male relatives, and immediate dependents. Others, unrelated to the family, when joining a band of warriors, were known as *kenin* (retainers), a word which has the literal meaning of 'people living in the house'. Fortified by their warbands, the provincial barons—whether or not they happened to be the official agents of the Heian court—were in a position either to act as the arm of the government, in the suppression of rebellion, for example, or to ignore, and even defy, edicts from Kyoto. This state of affairs existed at least as early as the end of the ninth century. At that time numerous orders and prohibitions complaining of abuses were issued by the government but never obeyed. The situation is well summed up by Sir George Sansom: 'Characteristically these documents (government edicts) dwell in Confucian fashion upon the ethical aspect of the case, and deplore the corruption of public morals which follows such behaviour. But what they are really condemning is the rise of a military class, which had already begun to exercise real power at an even earlier date, when provincial governors on the expiry of their term of office would elect to remain in the country, there to found country families living on large estates and always, as their households grew, looking out for more land.'[3]

In the first half of the tenth century there was a striking demonstration of the power of the new class. In 935 Taira Masakado, already the controller of large estates in the east, expanded his territory by force and soon came into open rebellion against Kyoto. He even went so far as to proclaim himself 'the new emperor'. He was in fact a distant kinsman of the imperial house, being descended from the Emperor Kammu (781–806). Pedigree was an important factor in medieval Japan; it lent an air of legitimacy to naked power. Thus Masakado's pretensions could not be regarded, in the east at any rate, as wholly improper.

The rebellion was suppressed only after some five years of warfare, in which the Kyoto government had to rely on the services of other provincial fighting men. The army which subdued Masakado was in fact commanded by his first cousin, another Taira, whose motive for obeying Kyoto was at least in part the desire to carry out a personal vendetta, since his father had been killed by Masakado. Thus the private troops of local lords, the despised family warbands, had decided the outcome in a war affecting the imperial succession.

By the middle of the eleventh century whole provinces had been taken over by warrior lords and their retainers, but now they had begun to play a role of importance in Kyoto itself; to an increasing extent they manned the imperial guards and police. Rough men from the provinces, it was found, were the most effective defenders of the city's peace and order. They were particularly needed when, as often happened, local monks from the Buddhist fanes that dotted the hills above Kyoto entered the imperial city, armed to the teeth, to air their grievances.

It was in the eleventh century that two warrior houses, the Taira and Minamoto, emerged as leaders of what we can now begin to call samurai society. The Taira could boast of imperial descent, and the same was true of the Minamoto, whose exalted ancestor was the Emperor Seiwa (858–867). Because of readings of the Chinese ideographs, the Minamoto are also known as the Genji and the Taira as the Heishi, or Heike. By an elision of the two names the term, Gempei, is commonly used to refer to the Minamoto–Taira relationship, and their conflict in the late twelfth century is known as the Gempei War.

These two military houses were split into various branches. Thanks to Masakado's ambitions, one branch of the Taira had achieved great prominence and notoriety in the east, in the Kantō region. But in later years, specifically in the twelfth century, the base of Taira power was along both sides of the Inland Sea in western Japan; their considerable influence in the east and north had been greatly diminished by the action of their Minamoto rivals. By contrast, the Minamoto first attained power as reliable servants of the imperial court, which for most of the Heian age was manipulated by a gifted noble family, the Fujiwara. During the tenth century there was in effect a Fujiwara–Minamoto alliance in which the Minamoto were the junior, warlike, partners. Some of them served their senior colleagues so well, in fact, that they earned from their enemies the sobriquet of 'running dogs of the Fujiwara'.

It would be misleading to suppose that, as samurai, the Minamoto chiefs who served in Kyoto were totally devoid of the attributes of the courtier. They were not necessarily strangers to the arts of poetry and other civilized skills, but they were at the same time undeniably warriors, ready always to kill or be killed.

It was this stark spirit which distinguished the samurai, however well mannered and artistic he might be, from the courtier. Kyoto culture was essentially pacific: the death penalty, for example, was almost unknown, and severe punishments were uncommon. In short, bloodshed was distasteful to the imperial house and the Fujiwara-dominated court nobility. But no government, however humane and fastidious, can eschew the use of force, and to handle the harsher demands of administration it seemed fitting to employ the warrior class. By the tenth century the samurai had become, as the Japanese saying had it, 'the teeth and claws of the Fujiwara'.

In the eleventh century the Minamoto created for themselves a new territorial base in the Kantō, the region formerly dominated by the Taira under Masakado. The process had started with the suppression of another Taira revolt by a Minamoto commander acting for the court and government. There followed thereafter a remarkable extension of Minamoto power into northern Japan as a result of two extremely bitter wars against recalcitrant provincial chiefs. The terrain of these wars was unusually wild and inhospitable, and the fighting—often amid the deep snows of winter—peculiarly desperate. It has been suggested that it was during this fighting that the warrior's code of behaviour was 'formed and tested'.[4] Certainly the memory of the campaigns in the north was an inspiration to later generations of the Minamoto.

Among such memories was that of the shining figure of Minamoto Yoshie, a brilliant captain who won fame when hardly more than a boy and lived on, as a great clan chief, to what was then the ripe old age of 67. In his lifetime, he built up the moral and material fortunes of his house to a degree that alarmed the Kyoto court. In the eyes of his retainers and allies Yoshie well deserved his popular title of *Hachiman Tarō*, 'firstborn of the God of War'. The Ainu of the north, it was said, trembled at the very mention of his name. To his own descendants over the centuries he was the supreme family *Kami*.

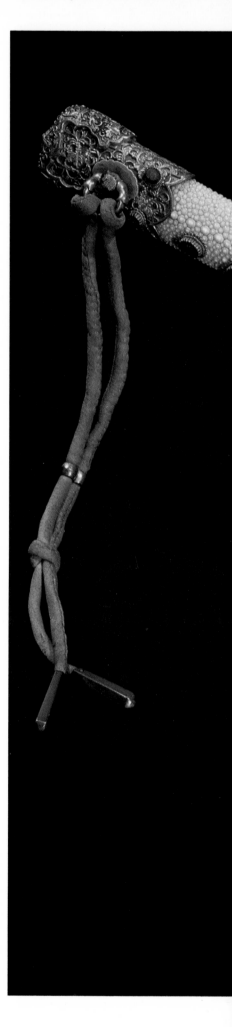

Right : This eighteenth-century samurai sword was made in deliberate imitation of a sword of the Heian era, with elaborate enamel and gilt work

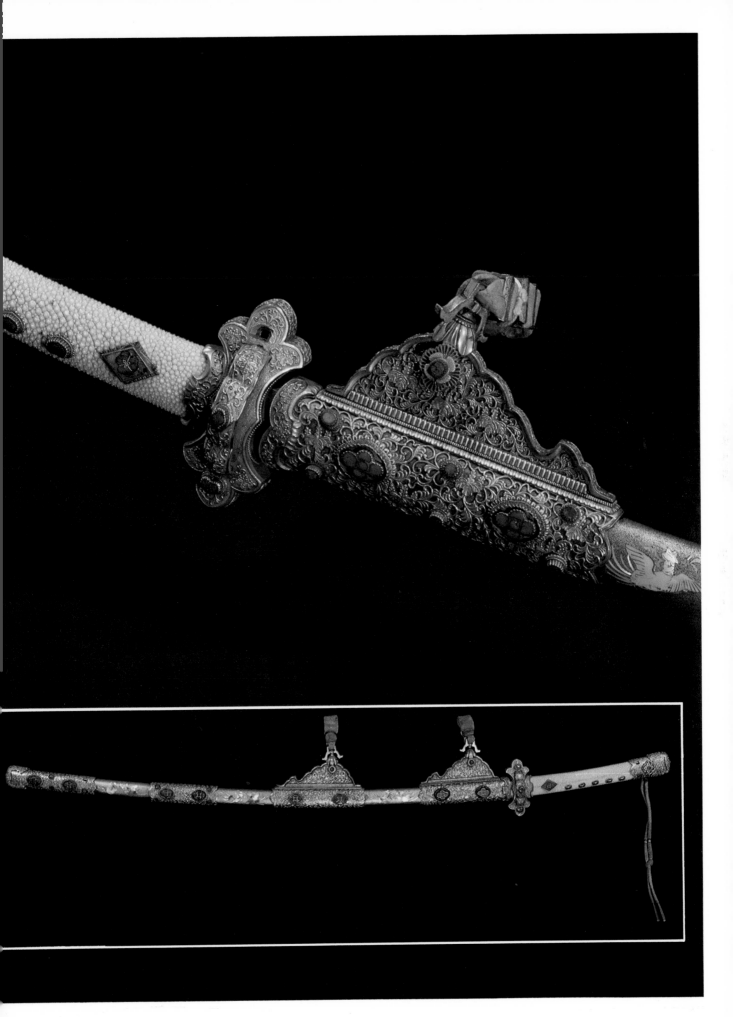

Above and above right: Two further scenes from the scroll depicting the Heiji Insurrection. Painted in the middle of the Kamakura period, this scroll reflects the contemporary veneration for heroes and military action. The style is vivid and captures much of the excitement of the historic struggle in the streets of Kyoto during which the Taira confirmed their position as the first samurai family to rule in Japan

The personal qualities of a war leader such as Minamoto Yoshie were powerful factors in attracting men to his standard. But loyalty was not always divorced from considerations of self-interest; faithful retainers also had the right to expect some reward at the conclusion of a victorious campaign, such as a share in the property of the vanquished. After the heads of enemy leaders had been despatched with proper ceremony for inspection in Kyoto—as proof of victory—came the distribution of enemy lands to faithful allies and loyal house carls. Yoshie was notably punctilious in satisfying such obligations. It is not cynical to suggest that it was this, as much as his tactical skill and martial ardour, that bound men to his service.

Service, at all events, came to be the heart of the warrior's ethical code. The very word *samurai* is written with an ideograph which means 'one who serves'. Those at the apex of the samurai order, such as the leaders of the Minamoto and Taira, thought of themselves as serving the *Tennō*, the emperor, whom they cherished in their imagination as a symbolic and immaculate figure, irrespective of the particular character and personality of the man, or child, who happened to occupy the throne. Subjectively, therefore, the samurai class, when it eventually thrust its way to supreme political power in the twelfth century, was scarcely conscious of having usurped the authority of the imperial court.

Yet that is what happened. And those who first seized the levers of power were not the Minamoto, as might have been expected, but their rivals, the Taira.

In the east the Taira had lost ground, in every sense, to the Minamoto; but while Yoshie was consolidating his victories, branches of the Taira house were building and extending a secure base from Ise, south of Nagoya, westward as far as Kyushu. In these operations the principal

figures were Taira Masamori and his son, Tadamori. It was Tadamori's son, Taira Kiyomori, who was the first to achieve for the warrior order the political supremacy which, in one form or another, it retained up to modern times.

This extremely significant shift in the balance of power occurred in 156, when an ugly affair known as the *Hōgen-no-Ran* ('the Hōgen year-period Insurrection') erupted in the capital. Its background is complicated and need not concern us here. Put most simply, a dispute arose within the imperial family with rival members of the Fujiwara on opposing sides. The quarrel deteriorated into armed conflict, resolved in a night battle, in which Taira and Minamoto fought on both sides, close relatives in combat with one another. But the outcome left only one prominent Minamoto captain, Yoshitomo, in any position of influence in Kyoto. It was Taira Kiyomori who emerged as the dominant figure. Symbolic of the new regime were the public executions of some of the defeated leaders, the first executions openly carried out in Kyoto for more than 300 years.

Taira Kiyomori then began to draw into his own hands the reins of government, arranging such matters as the imperial succession and manipulating Fujiwara courtiers and officials at will. Three years after the Hōgen affair another clash of arms provided him with the opportunity of eliminating any remaining Minamoto challenge to his power in Kyoto. Minamoto Yoshitomo, taking advantage of a temporary absence of Kiyomori from the capital, carried out a *coup d'état* in collaboration with a disaffected young Fujiwara nobleman. The fighting that ensued is known as the *Heiji-no-Ran,* or the Heiji Insurrection (Heiji being the name given to the era). A more dramatic and prolonged affair than the brief Hōgen Insurrection it was, nevertheless, all over in about a month.

On hearing of the *coup* Kiyomori hurried back to Kyoto, and when battle was joined there was a good deal of hard fighting with much destruction of the elegant buildings of the capital. Some of these episodes are portrayed in the thirteenth-century Heiji Monogatari picture scroll.

The rout of the Minamoto was complete, though a few, including Yoshitomo, contrived to escape. They hoped to reach safety in the east and to rally support there. It was the winter season, and snowstorms made their flight exceedingly difficult. With Yoshitomo were three of his many sons. One of them, aged 15, had been wounded in the fighting and could not keep up with the others. Dreading the shame of capture, he implored his father to kill him. Having put him to death, Yoshitomo himself did not long survive: he was killed by a treacherous retainer. Of the other two boys one was the eleven-year-old Yoritomo, the future architect of the Kamakura shogunate. A magisterial figure of great importance in Japan's history, Yoritomo was lucky indeed not to have shared his father's fate. He fell instead into the hands of a Taira captain who took pity on him and persuaded Taira Kiyomori (through the mediation of Kiyomori's step-mother) to spare the boy's life. Behaving in this instance more like a civilized courtier than a merciless warrior, Kiyomori gave orders for Yoritomo to be banished to the Izu peninsula, far away in the east.

The youngest of Yoshitomo's sons was still an infant. This was Yoshitsune, born of a concubine called Tokiwa, a court lady famous for her beauty. Tokiwa and the child, with two further boys of hers by Yoshitomo were captured and brought before Kiyomori. The story goes that he offered to spare their lives if Tokiwa agreed to become his mistress and send her three sons to Buddhist temples to be trained as monks. In later years it became part of samurai folklore that Kiyomori's dream of a night of bliss had brought ruin to his house. For within 25 years the Taira were to be utterly destroyed; and the destruction, planned by Yoritomo, would be carried out by Yoshitsune.

Thus the mercy shown to two children of the Minamoto, Yoritomo and his half-brother Yoshitsune, was seen by successive generations of the samurai order as a noble or foolish, but in any case fatal, mistake. This brutal lesson, one must sadly record, seems to have been well learned, providing a justification for infanticide in later civil wars.

All accounts appear to emphasize the pride and arrogance of the Taira in their heyday. Kiyomori, evidently determined to match his political power with social prestige, secured for himself the highest court rank—a

Above : A house built in the Kamakura period for a samurai family named Hakogi. The Hakogi became ronin, or samurai who owed allegiance to no feudal lord.
Above right : A detail from the Heiji illustrated scroll depicting Minamoto Yoshitomo at the beginning of the Heiji Insurrection. His own role was to lead to tragic defeat but his sons, Yoritomo and Yoshitsune, were to establish Minamoto power and avenge his defeat

most exceptional distinction for a warrior, even if he was of imperial descent—and in general he adopted the life-style of a Fujiwara nobleman. He ruled Kyoto like a dictator; but we have to bear in mind that even during periods when the samurai class was most assertive, was indeed all powerful, the imperial court and government always retained a certain irreducible prestige. In the attitude of the *bushi*—the warriors—to the Kyoto court aristocracy, throughout the medieval age, there seems to have persisted a feeling of inferiority which the nobles themselves, with their often unconcealed contempt for samurai manners, did little to alleviate.

It was through intermarriage with the imperial line that the Fujiwara had originally established and maintained their long ascendancy at court. Taking a leaf from their book, Kiyomori married off his daughter to an

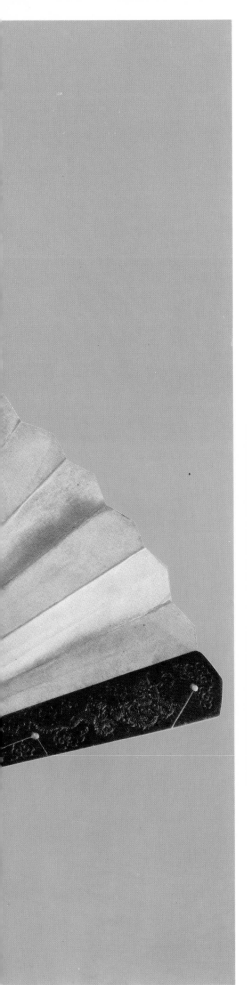

emperor, and in 1180 he had the ineffable satisfaction of seeing his three-year old grandson ascend the throne as the Emperor Antoku, Japan's 81st sovereign. But by that year Kiyomori was over 60 years old, and in failing health. He had not long to live, and his last months were darkened by anxieties: there had been a serious, if abortive, conspiracy in the capital and there was bad news from the east.

These were the first signs that mark the beginning of the Gempei War of 1180–1185, an epic struggle famous in history and legend, providing for future generations a rich storehouse of romantic tales, some authentic, others largely or entirely apocryphal. A huge literature was to grow up round the events and personalities of the war. It may be said to constitute the Japanese equivalent of the Arthurian Legend combined with echoes from the world of Robin Hood. The Gempei War has supplied the plots for Noh drama, puppet drama, Kabuki plays and, in modern times, of innumerable films. The white banners of the victorious Genji (Minamoto) and the red of the vanquished Heike (Taira) can be seen today on school and college playing fields from Nemuro to Kagoshima as the colours of contending teams.

The main features of the Gempei War, in terms of the known historical facts, are sufficiently colourful and dramatic in themselves without any of the fictional elaboration that has grown around them. The legends, however, illustrate various facets of what was to become part of the samurai tradition.

The proximate origin of the struggle was a plot hatched in Kyoto by a

*When folded, a war fan's iron
endplates could be used as a weapon
or parrying device.
Left: Each side of this fan carries the
military device of the sun disc, while
the endplates are decorated with
zodiacal animals and gold inlay.
Above: A sixteenth-century door
painting showing a samurai in action
carrying a war fan*

disgruntled Minamoto veteran named Yorimasa, described by Sansom as 'a warrior wearing Court robes'. Yorimasa had been passive during the Heiji Insurrection, though he seemed to be on the side of the Taira. In subsequent years he came to be regarded by Kiyomori as wholly reliable. By 1180 he was 77 years of age, and it was taken for granted that he presented no possible threat to the Taira oligarchy. He had some fame as a poet, and Kiyomori appears to have thought well of him. But this old man harboured intense secret resentments, for he had once been gravely insulted by Kiyomori's son. Not only that: it seems that he was often made the butt of jokes by the Taira.[5]

A recurring feature in any history of the samurai is the great importance that a warrior attached to the repayment of debts—of vengeance as well as gratitude. A personal humiliation, even when caused unintentionally, could not be overlooked; it must be wiped out sooner or later, however long the injured party had to wait. In Francis Bacon's words, 'a man that studieth revenge keeps his own wounds green'.

Such was Yorimasa's frame of mind when, early in 1180, he got in touch with a prince of the imperial house who had his own reasons for detesting the Taira, since he had twice been bypassed for the succession, the second occasion being the enthronement of Kiyomori's grandchild, Antoku. Yorimasa persuaded the prince to send a call to arms to Minamoto leaders in the east; it being understood that after the overthrow of the Taira the prince would ascend the throne. This secret summons reached Minamoto Yoritomo in Izu within three weeks.

Kiyomori, however, got wind of the conspiracy, and the prince fled from Kyoto, soon to be joined by Yorimasa, the male members of his family, and a small force of retainers. They believed the monks of Tōdai-ji at Nara—a well-armed group cherishing grudges of its own against Kiyomori—would afford them protection pending help from the Minamoto in the east. The party had got as far as Uji, between Kyoto and Nara, when they were overtaken by a Taira host, said to have numbered 20,000, although this figure is no doubt exaggerated.

The climax of the ensuing hopeless battle took place close to the Byōdō-in, an elegant villa built by a Fujiwara minister and converted into a monastery. In the last stages of the fight Yorimasa rode off with the prince, for whose safety he was responsible, but he was struck by an enemy arrow. Urging the prince to continue his flight, the old man turned back to the Byōdō-in. There, just in front of the graceful central pavilion, the Phoenix Hall (today the largest surviving building of the Heian age) Yorimasa, kneeling on his iron fan, disembowelled himself with his own sword.

The bloody scene of the old warrior's *hara-kiri* in front of the Phoenix Hall is said to be the second on record, the first having occurred in 1170, with the self-immolation of another Minamoto captain. Doubtless there were earlier examples. There may have been one or two cases in Yoshie's campaigns in the north during the previous century.

The odd fact is that nobody seems to know the precise origins of this excruciatingly painful form of suicide. But *seppuku* (reckoned to be the more dignified reading of the two ideographs for *hara-kiri*, 'cutting of the belly') became in due course the means of death in four different sets of circumstances. It was resorted to in order to avoid unutterable disgrace, such as capture by the enemy, as in the case of Yorimasa. It could also be performed as an act of *junshi*, suicide on the death of one's lord; or it was the ultimate way of remonstrating with an erring superior. Finally, it was the capital sentence imposed on a warrior by the authorities. *Hara-kiri* was of course the prerogative of the samurai class. Priests, peasants, artisans, and traders were neither expected nor allowed to choose this means of self-destruction. A Kyoto nobleman, for instance, might take poison.

This certainly suggests that *hara-kiri* was adopted primarily because it was a demonstration of almost superhuman courage, the quality which

Below: One of the victims of the Gempei wars was the Tōdai-ji at Nara. This group of Buddhist buildings was destroyed by the Taira clan in 1180 because of the armed monks' collaboration with the Minamoto cause. When Minamoto Yoritomo emerged victorious he had the Tōdai-ji rebuilt. All that remains of his work is the great south gate or Nandaimon. Designed by a member of the Jōdo (Pure Land) sect, it is a fine example of the new architecture of the early Kamakura period

anked with loyalty as the highest, indispensable virtue of the samurai. As one authority has suggested: 'This choice of extreme suffering was no doubt related . . . to the idea that it was incumbent on members of the *lite* warrior class to display their unique courage and determination by undergoing an agonizing ordeal that mere commoners (or women) could not possibly endure'.[6]

It is also the case that in Japan the abdomen *(hara)* was thought to be the very core of a man's being, in which were stored his spirit, will and emotions. And the samurai must be prepared if necessary to show his sincerity by exposing that core. A passage from Mishima's *Sun & Steel* is a somewhat bizarre reflection of this particular obsession:

'Let us picture a single, healthy apple . . . The inside of the apple is naturally quite invisible. Thus at the heart of that apple, shut up within the flesh of the fruit, the core lurks in its wan darkness, tremblingly anxious to find some way to reassure itself that it is a perfect apple. The apple certainly exists, but to the core this existence as yet seems inadequate; if words cannot endorse it, then the only way to endorse it is with the

eyes. Indeed, for the core the only sure mode of existence is to exist and to see at the same time. There is only one method of solving this contradiction. It is for a knife to be plunged deep into the apple so that it is split open and the core is exposed to the light—to the same light, that is, as the surface skin. Yet then the existence of the cut apple falls into fragments; the core of the apple sacrifices existence for the sake of seeing.'[7]

In due course death by *seppuku* was perceived to be not only courageous but also 'beautiful', since it was an honourable and therefore aesthetically satisfying end to a life, however short, of dedicated service. From at least the beginning of the thirteenth century *seppuku* as a practical contingency became so much a part of the samurai tradition that a warrior's son was given theoretical instruction in the method before he reached manhood.

In later years *seppuku* acquired the form of a ceremonial ritual, notably when a samurai was ordered by his superiors (either the government or his own feudal lord) to commit suicide. By the late seventeenth century elaborate rules and customs existed to cover the approved procedure in such cases. There were stipulations, for example, as to the number and arrangement of the *tatami* to be used. *Tatami* were the portable reed mats measuring about one metre by two (three by six feet) used as coverings for the floors of most homes. It was also stipulated that they be edged with white, and upon them must be placed a large white cushion on which the principal actor, the warrior about to commit *seppuku*, would place himself in formal style, kneeling with his body resting on his heels

Left and above: Musicians in a performance of Gagaku, the ancient court music of Japan. Introduced from Korea and China during the seventh and eighth centuries AD, Gagaku and Bugaku – the dance associated with it – were quickly assimilated into Shinto rites. They thus came under the special patronage of the emperor and have remained so ever since. Even when the samurai had usurped the power of the emperor and the Kamakura Bakufu had been established, imperial patronage was required for the continuation of many of the Japanese traditions

Just over one metre to his left, and to his rear, knelt the *kaishaku-nin,* the assistant at *seppuku,* who should be a close friend of the principal. The *kaishaku-nin* held a drawn sword in both hands. It was his function to decapitate the principal at a moment to be agreed between the two of them before the ceremony started. The word *kaishaku* means to attend or to serve, and the function of the *kaishaku-nin* was essentially merciful, namely, to spare the principal unnecessary agony. Thus, unless specifically instructed otherwise by his friend, the *kaishaku-nin* watched intently for the slightest indication of pain or irresolution, ready to strike off the head of the condemned warrior as soon as the latter had picked up the dirk from the tray in front of him and plunged it into his flesh.

It seems that on many occasions the decapitation took place at the instant when the dirk was picked up from the tray, or even when the principal stretched his hand towards the dirk. This still counted as an official *seppuku.* For those courageous enough to go through with the ordeal, the full ritual involved the cutting of the abdomen from left to right, followed by a slight cut upwards at the end. This was known as the *jūmonji,* the crosswise cut. When this was done the *kaishaku-nin* would perform his act of mercy.

There is a classic account of a *seppuku* written by an Englishman who witnessed the ceremony. It took place early in 1868, at the very end of the feudal era, and was performed at night in a temple near Kobe, the principal being a samurai named Taki Zenzaburō who had been condemned for ordering his men to fire on foreigners in the Kobe settlement. A. B. Mitford (later the first Lord Redesdale) attended the *seppuku* as the representative of the British Legation.

'Deliberately, with a steady hand, he took the dirk that lay before him; he looked at it wistfully, almost affectionately; for a moment he seemed to collect his thoughts for the last time, and then stabbing himself deeply below the waist on the left-hand side, he drew the dirk slowly across to the right side, and, turning it in the wound, gave a slight cut upwards. During this sickeningly painful operation he never moved a muscle of his face. When he drew out the dirk, he leaned forward and stretched out his neck . . . At that moment the *kaishaku,* who, still crouching by his side, had been keenly watching his every movement, sprang to his feet, poised his sword for a second in the air; there was a flash, a heavy, ugly thud, a crashing fall; with one blow the head had been severed from the body.'[8]

If it became second nature for a self-respecting samurai to regard death 'as lighter than a feather', the manner of death, the style with which his last encounter was handled, was always seen, particularly in times of trouble, as crucial in any assessment of a warrior's career. It is not surprising that the act of *seppuku,* under its more commonly recognized name of *hara-kiri,* should be the single fact about the samurai most widely known beyond Japan's shores.

The blood at the portals of the Phoenix Hall, which was defilement to the Fujiwara, was a badge of honour for the samurai, Minamoto and Taira alike. Such was the temper of those who had intruded into the fastidious world of the Heian court.

Kiyomori, heartened as he might have been by the rapid suppression of Yorimasa's revolt, was soon disturbed by reports reaching him from the east. Yoritomo had contrived, after some initial setbacks, to raise a considerable army of the Minamoto and their allies, among whom were certain branches of the Taira at variance with their kinsmen in Kyoto and western Japan.

Yoritomo's exile in Izu had been a comfortable affair. Supposedly a political prisoner, he had come to enjoy more or less complete freedom, winning the regard and indeed the eventual loyalty of the local lord,

Hōjō Tokimasa, commissioned to keep an eye on him. This was the more remarkable in that he had eloped with Tokimasa's daughter on the eve of her wedding to another man. However, she married Yoritomo with her father's blessing; and Tokimasa, despite his own family links with the Taira, became Yoritomo's own vassal and close confidant. Hōjō Tokimasa was an unusually astute, far-sighted warrior; and his daughter Masa, Yoritomo's wife, was a commanding personality in her own right. Their joint influence on Yoritomo was considerable, and without his father-in-law's backing it is doubtful whether Yoritomo could have embarked upon the venture that would make him the master of Japan.

Kiyomori had dispatched a formidable army against the east, one that outnumbered Yoritomo's own force. On the plain stretching from the foot of Mount Fuji, the two samurai hosts faced each other across the Fujikawa river. Yet the expected battle to the death never occurred. After some skirmishing the Taira army withdrew in haste to the west. According to the *Azuma Kagami (Mirror of the East)*, a history compiled about a century after the events it describes, the Taira were thrown into unseemly panic by noise of frightened flocks of birds from the river marshes disturbed at night by an enemy reconnaissance party. The sound of the flapping wings, it was said, resembled that of a huge army on the march; and before dawn the Taira had begun their retreat. Yoritomo and his commanders did not pursue them. They still had potential enemies in their rear. Yoritomo now established his headquarters at Kamakura, the decision being taken to unify the east before pressing forward against the Taira in the west.

In March 1181, four months after the Fujikawa debacle, Taira Kiyomori died. Legend has it that on his death-bed he made his sons and grandsons swear to leave Yoritomo's corpse rotting on the ground.

Kamakura was chosen by Yoritomo as his seat of power.
Above: At the Sugimoto-dera, said to be the oldest temple in Kamakura, tombstones standing on the hillside commemorate this site of many battles.
Right: This giant bronze statue of the Buddha in Kamakura was created under the patronage of members of Yoritomo's entourage in 1252

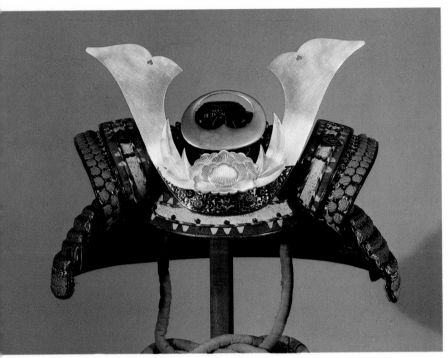

In the following two years there was little actual fighting between Minamoto and Taira; both sides exerted themselves to win the support of the uncommitted. Much of Yoritomo's time was occupied with turning Kamakura, described in the *Azuma Kagami* as 'a secluded place . . . frequented only by fishermen and aged rustics', into a thriving town to house and serve his family, his phalanx of retainers, and the growing number of those who came forward with pledges of allegiance. From the beginning, the building of shrines, temples and impressive residences implied that Kamakura was to be much more than a mere temporary headquarters for the Minamoto in the east. Indeed, Yoritomo set up something very like a royal court, complete with ceremonial obligations which his vassals would be expected to observe. Nobody, needless to say, thought of these developments as an infringement on the authority of the Kyoto court, much less as the creation of a rival establishment. But in fact a new structure of government was in the process of being born.

The Gempei struggle was renewed on a large scale in the spring of 1183. It is unnecessary to follow all the ramifications, the ebb and flow, of the fighting in the various campaigns that preceded the final overthrow of the Taira in April 1185. All that needs to be said is that the Kantō *bushi*, the eastern warriors, achieved their ultimate victory above all as a result of three famous battles, in which Yoritomo's young half-brother, Yoshitsune, played the leading role.

Yoritomo, meanwhile, remained in the east, directing his generals from a distance, in the style of supreme commander, almost as much concerned with problems of economic organization and political finesse as with those of strategy. The Kantō was by far the most productive agricultural region of Japan. This heartland of the samurai, under Yoritomo's firm control, supplied the great armies he sent into the field.

The first of the three Minamoto victories took place in February 1184 at a spot, now swallowed up by the modern port of Kobe, called Ichino-tani. Here the Taira had constructed a seemingly impregnable defensive position, across a very narrow strip of land between the mountains and the sea. But by an extraordinarily bold move Yoshitsune led less than 100 chosen men, at night, with their horses, up almost precipitous slopes to a ridge high above the Taira camp. Then, after daylight, while the Taira were repelling a frontal attack, Yoshitsune and his samurai came crashing down the steep hillside into the enemy, causing the utmost confusion among them. The Taira who survived had no choice but to escape in

The samurai of the Gempei war relied on two main weapons, the sword and bow. They were expert in the use of the bow from horseback.
Below: Arrows of the Muromachi period, mounted on an ornamental stand.
Right: Steel arrows of the Tokugawa period, made in several styles. The pierced arrowhead, third from the left, carries a Buddhist inscription.
Far right, below: Sixteenth-century painting from a sliding door depicting a samurai riding into battle carrying his bow

boats across the Inland Sea to their own headquarters at Yashima (th modern Takamatsu) on the northern shore of Shikoku.

The second battle occurred just over a year later, in February 118? Yoshitsune again demonstrated his genius for offensive action, an against the advice of other Minamoto commanders, he took a force sai to have numered no more than 150 warriors across the Inland Sea fron Honshu to Shikoku. They travelled in small boats at the height of gale, but he had gambled successfully on the hope that the wind woul drive his boats speedily to the opposite shore. After landing, this deter mined but tiny band rode through the night until they were in sight o Yashima, where the Taira were in strength and had in their care th infant Emperor Antoku, his mother and the imperial regalia.

Yoshitsune's little force attacked at dawn, against the flames of house they had put to the torch. It seems barely credible that the Taira, misle as they may have been by the fires and taken utterly by surprise, shoul have surrendered to panic. Yet they hastened to their ships, with th boy emperor, Antoku Tennō in their midst, and sailed towards th western end of the Inland Sea.

Little more than a month later, on 25 April, 1185, the last battle of th Gempei War took place off Dan-no-ura on the Honshu shore of the Inlan Sea, not far from Shimonoseki. It was a sea fight. Yet again, Yoshitsune' offensive spirit carried the day. In a matter of hours the Taira were no only defeated but exterminated. Among those drowned was Antok Tennō.

The ghosts of the Taira (the Heike) were said to haunt the scene o their defeat. A folktale familiar to every child in Japan records that th large crabs known as *Heike-gani*, harvested in the Shimonoseki Straits ir earlier, industrially unpolluted, days, bore on their shells the marking of samurai war helments; for these crustacea were the reincarnated soul of the arrogant Heike slain or drowned in their thousands off Dan-no-ura

Of the many legends surrounding the Gempei War, the most poten and numerous focus on Yoshitsune. It has been rightly observed tha 'though Yoshitsune made not the slightest contribution to the advance ment of society or culture, he is one of the most illustrious and beloved personalities in Japanese history'.[9] The tragedy of Yoshitsune lay in the fact that in spite of, or perhaps because of, his brilliant success as a commander in battle he became the object of Yoritomo's implacable rancour; and it was not long before he was a fugitive on the run, hunted by his brother's myrmidons. He contrived, after many vicissitudes, to find haven and protection in the mountains of the north. But his hosts, under persistent pressure from Yoritomo in Kamakura, eventually turned against him. Yoritomo had extracted from Kyoto an imperial commission for Yoshitsune's arrest as a rebel, and finally, in the summer of 1189, the hero of Ichinotani, Yashima, and Dan-no-ura found himself surrounded and attacked by those who had sheltered him. In this extremity Yoshitsune committed suicide after killing his wife and children. His head, preserved in sweet saké in a black lacquer box, was duly sent south for inspection by Yoritomo's officers.

In the folklore surrounding Yoshitsune there is inevitably a good deal of sentimentality, as well as real poetical feeling. Inseparably associated with Yoshitsune, in legend at all events, is the figure of a roving, fighting, monk. This is Benkei, a man portrayed as physically enormous and immensely strong—Friar Tuck and Little John, we might say, rolled into one. Historically, it seems that such a person did exist, for his name finds occasional mention in the chronicles. But in the Yoshitsune legend he plays a most important role; and in some stories it is Benkei rather than Yoshitsune who occupies the centre of the stage. The briefest summary of two of the most famous episodes from the Yoshitsune–Benkei legend may convey something of the genre.

The two heroes first met, it is said, one night on the Gojō Bridge in

Kyoto. Here Benkei, armed with a huge halberd, stopped and demanded the submission of an elegant youth, hardly more than a young boy, attired in a woman's cloak and playing a flute. The boy, Yoshitsune, defying Benkei, resisted every attempt to subdue him, nimbly leaping out of harm's way every time the great halberd swept in his direction. Benkei was finally exhausted and outwitted. Accordingly, he swore eternal fealty to the young Yoshitsune. That scene, immortalized on stage and in pictorial representations of every kind, lives in the imagination of every Japanese.

The second episode—the subject of both a Noh drama and a very popular Kabuki adaptation—relates to the final, fugitive, period of Yoshitsune's life, when he and Benkei and a handful of devoted warriors are making their way in disguise to the mountains of the north. They are stopped at a barrier by an officer of Yoritomo's government. Benkei pretends that he is travelling to collect subscriptions for the repair of the Tōdai-ji temple at Nara. The men with him, including Yoshitsune, are disguised as porters. Yoritomo's officer, suspicious of the party, puts Benkei to the test by asking him to read out the names of those who are subscribing money for the work at Nara. Undismayed, Benkei unfolds a scroll of blank paper and, drawing on his own spontaneous inventiveness, reads aloud a multitude of names and other particulars, including many recondite allusions to the Tōdai-ji and its history. Yoritomo's man, whose name is Togashi, allows the party to proceed; but as the porters go by he recognizes one of them as Yoshitsune, and says so at once. Benkei turns back and savagely beats Yoshitsune, cursing him for an impudent fool of a porter. How dare he resemble Yoshitsune!

Togashi, Yamamoto's officer, then declares that he must have been mistaken; he tells Benkei that they can resume their journey. Once beyond the barrier and out of sight of Togashi, Benkei in tears begs Yoshitsune for his forgiveness, while Yoshitsune, also in tears, thanks Benkei for saving his life. At that moment Togashi sends for them again, offering wine by way of apology. Benkei performs a dance, pretending to be drunk; he indicates, with his eyes, that the porters should depart. He then follows them, the last to leave.

This celebrated episode—portrayed regularly on the Kabuki stage as *Kanjin-chō (The Subscription List)*—illustrates certain aspects of ideal samurai behaviour as perceived many years later, for although the Noh version of this story dates from the fifteenth century, the Kabuki was not presented until the early nineteenth century.

Benkei's breach of etiquette, when he thrashes his master, Yoshitsune, is, of course, not only forgivable but also essential. Nevertheless, it is deeply shocking—not least to Benkei himself. It is the clearest proof to the suspicious Togashi that the porter cannot possibly be a samurai.

However, there is a further significance to the story. As performed on the stage it is made clear to the audience, although of course in no obvious sense, that not only does Togashi suspect that Benkei is inventing the names of subscribers but also he perceives that the porter is indeed Yoshitsune. He is ineffably impressed, nevertheless, by Benkei's assault on Yoshitsune, and by Yoshitsune's passive acceptance of this punishment. So, although he realizes the porter's true identity, he is moved to a merciful sympathy and allows them all to continue the journey north. This indeed is the reason why he offers wine. And at this point Benkei understands Togashi's attitude; both of them know, without saying a word, what is in each other's mind.

For magnanimous behaviour such as Togashi's there is an expression: *bushi-no-nasaké* (the sympathy or clemency of the warrior). This is close to the traditional European concept of chivalry in at least part of its meaning. The unspoken dialogue between Togashi and Benkei, moreover, illustrates what is known as *hara-gei,* literally 'stomach-play', or 'belly-art'. This is mutual understanding achieved, sometimes in a flash, by intuition, quite irrespective of what is actually said by one or

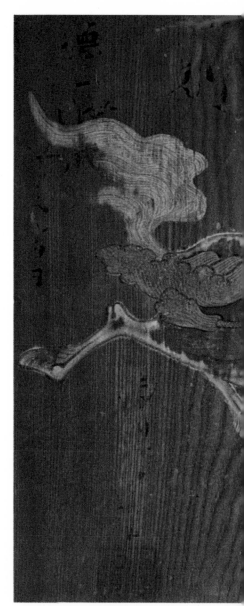

Below : A vigorous scene of personal combat between two warriors depicted in a votive painting from the Yasaka Shrine, Kyoto. It was a matter of great honour to be first to engage the enemy. Before any combat, the warrior would proudly recite his name and that of his forebears

ther of the two parties concerned. The effective operation of *hara-gei*
 not unrelated to Zen, a vital element in samurai culture from the early
hirteenth century onwards.

By the time the Gempei War had ended with the annihilation of the
Taira at Dan-no-ura, the distinctive ethos of the samurai was firmly
accepted on all sides. His armour, weapons, demeanour, his whole style
f life, separated the samurai from the rest of society. The typical samurai
vas a figure on horseback armed with bow and sword. The bow was used
vith remarkable dexterity, for the samurai had become adept at winging
is arrows from the saddle at full gallop. The sword was used in close
ork, when an opponent was unhorsed.

Great significance was attached to individual combat, to the man-to-
han clash between warriors of comparable rank and fame. This called
or a degree of punctilio even in the heat of battle. The warrior riding
into the fray would loudly announce his name and that of his ancestors;
e would challenge his enemies to produce a stalwart of equal merit and
ineage. It was normal indeed before battle started for a leading com-
ander on each side to advance and proclaim his pedigree.

Such was the colourful tradition consolidated during the Gempei
truggle. Once the war was over, Minamoto Yoritomo was faced with the
ess dramatic task of cementing the supremacy of the samurai order. At
he same time he had to hold it in check by regulating its affairs, codify
s administration, and link its fortunes with those of his own family.

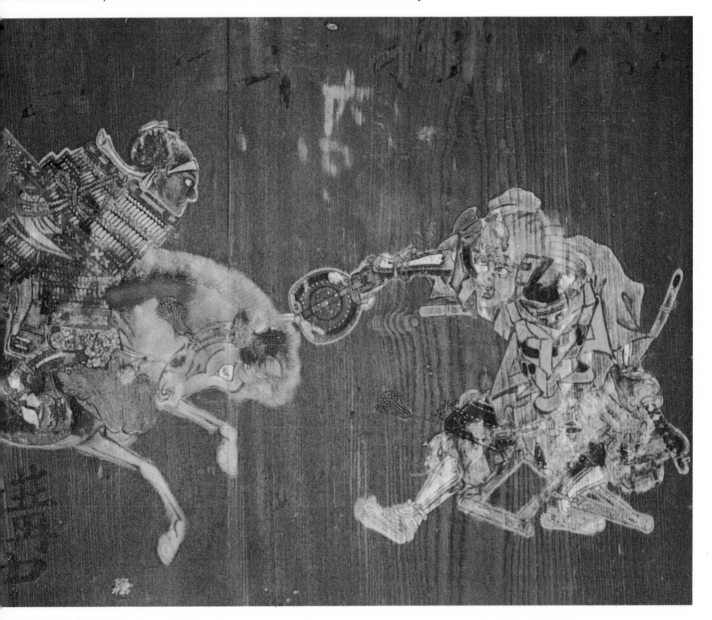

ZEN AND THE SWORD

The Kamakura, Muromachi and Momoyama periods

Left: The abbot of the Zen temple of Zuisen-ji, Kamakura, sits in quiet contemplation of the temple gardens. The gardens were designed by the temple's founder, Musō Kokushi, in 1327 and reflect the purest Zen style. By the astringent, balanced placing of the essential elements, stone, water and grasses, the garden conveys the quality of simplicity so important in the character of the samurai followers of Zen

In the last years of the twelfth century Yoritomo's headquarters at Kamakura became the seat of his military government or *Bakufu* (literally 'camp office'). He himself had obtained from Kyoto in 1192 the title of *Sei-i tai shōgun,* or 'Barbarian Suppressing Generalissimo'. The Bakufu was an administration of the samurai, by samurai, intended first and foremost for the samurai. In course of time, though in generations rather than decades, this type of military government became the basic pattern for the way in which the whole of Japan was ruled. But the imperial court, the old aristocracy of Kyoto, and the religious bodies retained for many years their political and economic hold over much of the country. The Kamakura Bakufu, however, soon demonstrated that it could provide an administrative and judicial organization more efficient, because less elaborate, than the traditional structure under the nominal authority of the sovereign emperor. It is important to stress once again that Yoritomo's government was not a usurpation of the imperial system but rather a legal expansion of specifically samurai power within that system. We have arrived, in other words, at the moment when the samurai is established as permanent political ruler, moral exemplar, and in many respects final arbiter of manners and taste.

The Kamakura Bakufu endured until 1334. Long before then it had ceased to be directed, save in name, by Yoritomo's descendants. Indeed, soon after his death in 1199 power passed into the hands of his widow's family, the Hōjō, and successive generations of that gifted warrior house held office as regents *(shikken)* for the shogun, who was himself no more than a figurehead, an interesting example of a double removal of power.

43

The Hōjō are the heroes of the Kamakura regime. For it was they who faced and overcame the unprecedented crisis of the two Mongol assaults of 1274 and 1281. These were beaten off thanks to the courage of the samurai armies mustered by the Hōjō, aided by what was regarded in a literal sense as the providential intervention of the elements. Severe gales during both invasions threw Kublai Khan's armada into disarray, though not before hordes of fighting men had come ashore. The second of these great storms, which almost wiped out the Mongol fleet, was known then and thereafter as the *Kamikaze*, 'The Divine Wind'.

After that ordeal Hōjō supremacy was maintained with increasing difficulty for another 50 years, but it was to end in 1333 with civil war. The enemies of the Hōjō attacked and overran Kamakura; whereupon the last Hōjō regent, his family, and some 800 retainers committed *seppuku* among the burning buildings. There ensued a period of dynastic confusion, and for a time there were competing courts, each headed by a rival emperor who belonged to the legitimate imperial line. Even when this struggle was eventually resolved lasting internal peace was little more than a dream. Indeed, until the closing years of the sixteenth century it seemed unlikely that a truly stable peace could ever be imposed and maintained by force for more than one or two decades.

Right: A cave at Kamakura, site of the dramatic end of the shogunate established by Yoritomo. Kamakura was taken by storm by the armies of Nitta Yoshisada. When the situation became hopeless the defenders —under the leadership of Hōjō Takatoki, the last Hōjō shikken or regent—retired to the Hōjō ancestral cemetery at the Tōshō-ji temple. There Takatoki, with all the members of his family and some 800 retainers, committed seppuku. In the centre stands his monument; as the samurai of highest rank he was the last to kill himself. It is said that one of the warriors, having drunk the customary cup of saké before suicide, cried: 'This gives a fine relish to the wine!' as he disembowelled himself.
Far right: During the Kamakura period a realistic style of sculpture developed. This is exemplified by this fearsome figure, one of the 12 sacred generals who were placed as guardians in one of the temples of Kyoto

The fall of the Hōjō meant the end of Kamakura as the seat of samurai government. A new shogunate was established in the Muromachi district of Kyoto, however, by the Ashikaga branch of the Minamoto. Ashikaga supremacy, in the political and military sense, was often more formal than real. Nevertheless, the Muromachi age (1339–1573) was one of great artistic merit, although it was marred by a series of bloody domestic wars, culminating in what became known as the *sengoku jidai,* 'the time of the country at war', during which there emerged the three great warriors—Nobunaga, Hideyoshi, and Ieyasu—who between them brought unity to a divided nation and laid the foundations of an enduring peace.

It was during the Kamakura Bakufu that Zen first imprinted itself on the psyche of the samurai. This school or sect of Buddhism, introduced into China from India by the patriarch Bodidharma in the sixth century reached Japan, it seems, about 100 years later but took no root in the country at that time. Its effective introduction dates from the end of the twelfth century, when it found its first true home in Kamakura, being welcomed and encouraged by the Hōjō.

In *The Book of Tea,* Okakura Kakuzō, citing a Ming author, observes that a translation 'can at its best be only the reverse side of a brocade— all the threads are there, but not the subtlety of colour or design'.[1] This

Left : The stone garden of the Ryōan-ji Temple in Kyoto, the quintessence of Zen. Fifteen stones, in five groups, rise from a rectangular 'sea' of white sand raked into a pattern each day. The wall behind has mellowed and weathered with the stones, and it is said that the garden is at its best when the stones and sand are wet from recent rain.
Below : A pond created in one of the earliest Zen gardens in Kyoto reflects the importance of water. The torii gateway is a Shinto motif, here adapted as an effective accent in the design of a Buddhist garden

applies with much greater force to even the most fastidious attempt to offer an intellectually comprehensible definition of the Enlightenment to be grasped through the practices of Zen. These call for an ascetic self-discipline. Everything else may be said to be superfluous, if not actually harmful. And, as one of the greatest modern authorities on Zen has pointed out: 'a good fighter is generally an ascetic or stoic, which means he has an iron will. This, when needed, Zen can supply'.[2] There is also the supreme importance which Zen gives to intuition, while rejecting the exercise of the rational and verbalizing intellect. The military mind is not as a rule much drawn to metaphysical speculation or philosophical debate; and these are eschewed by those who practice Zen. For Zen shows its power in action, its force and flavour being diminished once the element of explanation or analysis rears its head. Like riding a bicycle —which in theory sounds so difficult as to be almost impossible—Zen works; although not for everyone, and at times, perhaps, not for anyone.

The adept is one who has apprehended *Satori,* Enlightenment. A man can spend a lifetime in *Zazen,* Zen meditation, without grasping *Satori.* But this has never meant that there is no virtue, no real practical benefit, in shaping one's life in accordance with the unstated principles of Zen.

For Zen treats life and death indifferently: neither must be considered for a moment. It is essential only that a man should act wholeheartedly on the basis of whatever conclusion, rational or irrational, he has arrived at. There is here, then, an existentialist factor; and if Zen is any kind of religion it is a religion of the instinctive, uncluttered will operating in the Here and Now.

Thus the influence of Zen on the samurai was dramatic. It brought to the use of bow and sword an entirely new poise which, in an adept, could attain perfection. The samurai could be a notable iconoclast in his dealings with most Buddhist sects and beliefs. Bored by *Tendai* and *Shingon,* contemptuous of *Jōdo* (the 'Pure Land' faith embraced by the common people) the samurai recognized in the Zen masters men whose spirit was direct, hard and pure. Here was a faith, under the umbrella of Buddhism, that made demands not on the intellect, or on the emotions, but on the will or—to use another term—the moral fibre, the very source and stay of the warrior's pride. The most pragmatic and sceptical could perceive that some acquisition of the Zen spirit must give greater self-control, fortifying that superbly confident indifference to death which every samurai was expected to display.

There was something more. There was much in Zen that was congruous with the standards established and implied by the world of Shinto. The appeal here, we can say, was aesthetic rather than moral; although in Japan these terms are often interchangeable. The austerity of Zen, the sober unadorned nature of the Zen temples, and of the tea-houses inspired by the cult, may not have matched the overwhelming

mplicity of the Ise Shrines, but in basic taste the similarity was fairly
ose. Of course there remained certain important differences. Zen, after
l, was born of Buddhism. For all its rejection of holy texts, it bore the
atina of its ancestry. The simplicity of Shinto is wholly natural and
nforced. The simplicity of Zen is profound and subtle as those who
e the Ryōan-ji stone garden in Kyoto can readily understand.

There was another and possibly more important factor that made Zen
articularly acceptable to those whose lives were already deeply tinged
y Shinto. A central rite of Shinto is that of *harai,* 'purification'. At the
rdinary level this is symbolized by the visitor who rinses mouth and
ands at the water tank just inside the inner precincts of a shrine,
hether this happens to be Ise or merely a modest structure set among
e rice fields. Every kind of purification, from the simplest to the most
rmal, is intended to create or, more correctly, recreate in the Japanese
orshipper 'a clear, clean, heart'. There is in Shinto absolutely no con-
pt of Original Sin. A French scholar emphasizes the point: 'In Christian

treatises on morality, it is customary to deal with sin as the natural counterpart to virtue. That plurality does not exist in Shinto, where what we call sin is considered more in the nature of an extrinsic element, a mistake, which does not affect the real person.'³

A vital part in Zen training was directed to the release of a man's *honshō*, or 'true character'. This was a process not so much of building up as of stripping down, of sloughing off every outer element, until eventually a state of *Mu*, 'emptiness', 'void', 'no being', was attained. This is quite out of accord, needless to say, with the teachings of the Christian faith, which stresses the danger facing the soul that is 'swept and garnished', left vacant for Evil to return with added strength. But it is very close, if not identical with, esoteric practices of meditation known to Shinto.

The link between Shinto and Zen is rightly emphasized by the nationalist scholar, Fujisawa Chikao: 'A grasp of Zen Buddhism will pave the way for a thoroughgoing comprehension of Japanese traditional culture envisaged as a whole . . . But, few people are aware of the undeniable fact that Zen Buddhism was able to reach the culminating point of its development under the overwhelming influence of Shintoism, which constitutes permanently the kernel of the Japanese existential thought-pattern'.⁴

For the samurai, Shinto supplied the inherited ambience, Confucianism provided the ethical code, Zen shaped his style in peace and war. This peculiarly Japanese trinity was never symmetrical. The balance shifted according to fashion, historical period, local tradition, and individual vagaries. In our 'middle period' few warriors, perhaps, could see and assess this triple structure of influences with any clarity—or would have thought to do so.

The sword was the emblem of the samurai, the single most important element in his equipage.
Top: The swordsmith at work, from an artisan's screen.
Above: A tsuba or swordguard of th[e] Muromachi period with a simple design of fungus and bracken.
Right: A sword attributed to the famous Masamune (1264–1344), whose nobility of character is said to have pervaded his blades

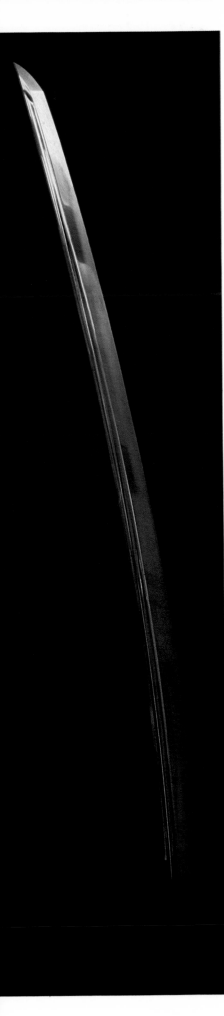

The making and handling of the warrior's sword illustrate the forces of the trinity at work. The making of a blade was an operation of religious solemnity, the master of the smithy purifying himself each day with ritual ablutions. He and his assistants heated and hammered, shut off from the world, until the finished blade was ready; and it was a process that could take many weeks to complete. From first to last it was pervaded by the ethos of Shinto. Once in the possession of the samurai the purpose of the sword was to further the service he owed to his lawful superior. Thus, loyal obligation was underpinned by the Confucian ethical code. The sword should not be drawn outside that context. But once drawn, the sword was handled in the spirit of Zen, the sure, most potent guide to its effective use.

For it was in swordsmanship above all that the manifestation of Zen was thought to be most significant. The two swords, long and short, thrust through the belt with the cutting edge uppermost were the most treasured material possessions of the samurai; they were the badge of his status and the symbol of his honour as a warrior. Zen could perfect the use of the bow, the spear, halberd, and (after the middle years of the sixteenth century) the smooth-bore musket. But from every point of view it was the sword, 'the soul of the samurai', that was supreme.

The cult of the sword in Japanese history and folklore is a huge subject in its own right. As an efficient cutting blade—none produced in any other part of the world can rival it—as a work of art, as a talisman, as a fetish, the sword of the samurai was held in unique esteem. In arrogant or brutal hands it could be a weapon of the utmost savagery, but it was also believed to be benign, even 'life-giving', in the hands of an adept who cherished *bushi-no-nasaké*, 'the warrior's sense of mercy and benevolence'.

A well-known story may serve here as an illustration. Muramasa, a brilliant but mentally unstable swordsmith enjoyed a somewhat sinister reputation, since his superb blades always tended to bring their owners into bloody conflict with others, with ultimate disaster for themselves. A man who wanted to test the mettle of a Muramasa sword placed one in a stream to see how it would react to the dead leaves floating on the current. Every leaf that touched the blade was cut cleanly in two. A sword made by the greatest of all swordsmiths, Masamune, was then placed in the stream. The leaves avoided the blade. This was said to reflect Masamune's own character; which had in it a measure of nobility. Indeed Masamune, recognized through the ages as the finest of all Japanese swordsmiths, rarely engraved his name on his hilts, although this practice was general among his contemporaries and successors. Thus the comment has been made: 'The Muramasa is terrible, the Masamune is humane.'[5]

In other words, a fine sword could be said to acquire the personality of the smith who made it. In some degree, therefore, it had an occult life of its own. From this hypothesis it follows that for the samurai who unsheathed his sword the condition known as *munen,* a Zen term of great antiquity and importance, was more than desirable; it was essential. *Munen,* meaning 'no thought', has been likened to the state of innocence enjoyed by the first inhabitants of Eden.[6] It should not, I imagine, be confused with *Satori,* Enlightenment, although *munen* is doubtless an indispensable step towards that goal. Some clarification of the meaning of *munen* is suggested by the Japanese phrase, *munen musō de aru,* 'to be free from all worldly cares'.

It cannot be emphasized too often that for the ideal warrior the way of the samurai was the way of death. There was great concern that the manner of death should reflect no stain of dishonour. Thus, to engage in combat with the slightest thought of possible death or injury to oneself was held to be calamitous. This of course is sound psychology, as personal experience will amply confirm. And we can readily appreciate the wisdom of the exhortation addressed to his followers by Uesugi Kenshin, one of the great captains of the sixteenth century: 'Go to the battlefield firmly confident of victory, and you will come home with no wounds whatever. Engage in combat fully determined to die and you will be alive; wish to survive in the battle and you will surely meet death. When you leave the house determined not to see it again you will come home safely; when you have any thought of returning you will not return.'[7]

For the accomplished swordsman even the thought of victory should not seep into his mind. His mind must be 'no mind' *(munen)*. Needless to say, such self-discipline could seldom be approached in reality, let alone attained, without prolonged and severe training.

The 'spiritual' properties of the sword were matched by its excellence as a work of art. The shallow curve, halfway between the straight blade of the European knight and the crescent shape of the Saracen scimitar, lends a unique grace to the weapon of the samurai. The surface displays what are called 'blade figures', an irregular pattern of great beauty, suggestive of the waves of the sea or mountainous crests, formed by various substances used in the process of firing and tempering. The hilt, scabbard, and sword-guard, are often of comparable beauty, and are usually decorated with designs taken from nature, representing flowers or birds.

Armour, too, from helmet to leg-guard was no less aesthetically pleasing. Most striking perhaps is the *kabuto,* the helmet. When horned or antlered it has an aspect both menacing and bizarre; and it is appropriate that the generic name for a beetle in Japanese should be *kabuto-mushi* ('helmet insect'), since the large black stag beetle, whose crustacean tegument and serrated mandibles closely resemble a miniscule version of the warrior's helmet, is commonly found in Japan.

The samurai's body armour demonstrates as great a regard for colour as for practical matters of protection and weight. In a memorable and characteristic passage Sacheverell Sitwell pays tribute to the colour and elaboration of Japanese medieval armour: 'The colour of Japanese armour depends upon the lacing; there is scarlet, or white laced armour, or purple lacing, like as many clans of coloured lobsters, but specialization, as always, is carried further still into silk braid of "rotted leaf colour", or deutzia blossom, or wistaria, or, of course, and almost tritely, cherry or pink plum blossom, and then, again, fern, or water plantain, or, more beautifully, jay's feather, it must be blue wing feather, lacing.'[8]

A complete suit of armour was reckoned to consist of at least 23 items, ranging from *fundoshi* (loin cloth) to *yari ate* (spear rest). But full armour

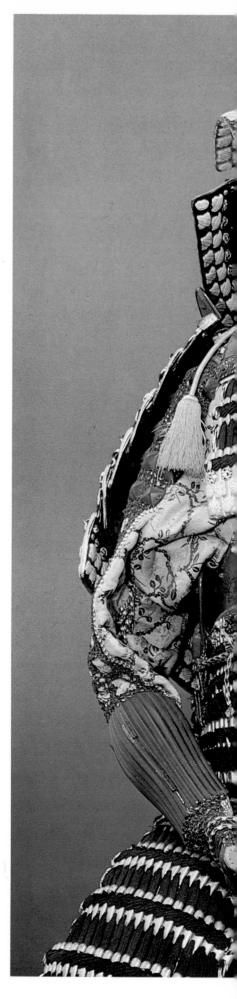

A samurai's armour consisted of at least 23 items, and his preparations for battle must have resembled those of a European knight.

Far left : The armourer at work, from an artisan's screen. Various pieces are being fashioned by the craftsman and apprentices, including helmets and body armour.

Left : An impressive suit of black armour in the Domaru *style of the late fourteenth century, one of the many styles used in the 700 years of samurai history. It incorporates pieces made by the* Myōchin *family of armourers.*

Above : Samurai armour from behind showing the agemaki *or large bow which held the shoulder plates in position. The coloured lacing was both decorative and allowed the warrior freedom of movement*

was often referred to by the term *roku gu*, six pieces: helmet, mask, body armour, thigh-pieces, gauntlets and leg-guards. Although armour underwent various changes during the feudal age, its basic style persisted more or less unaltered for some 700 years. A vast literature exists on armour, as it does on swords, most of it illustrated with detailed drawings and diagrams. A work of this type, when written for the use of samurai readers, discusses and makes recommendations on every article of the warrior's fighting gear and apparel. One such guide or manual, when dealing with the *hō-ate*, or mask, declares: 'A movable nose-piece is recommended. Whiskers on the mask are not particularly necessary, but it is desirable to have moustaches.'[9]

What was no doubt an optional item in the Samurai's equipment was the *kubibukoro*, or 'head bag', used to carry the severed head of an enemy. Nevertheless, the guide has something to say about it, and recommends: 'When walking, carry it hung to your waist, when mounted fasten it to the saddle'.[10]

One of the favourite maxims of the samurai, passed down from father to son, was: 'After victory tighten the strings of your helmet.' Thus the recreations thought proper for the warrior were those such as fencing and archery which tended to preserve a posture of alertness and vigilance.

But in course of time a less energetic but none the less important and valuable recreation (using this word in its real sense) won the allegiance of the samurai class. This was *cha-no-yu*, the Tea Ceremony. Inspired and developed by Zen monks, the ritual of the Tea Ceremony provided the samurai with a refreshment of the spirit that settled the mind before battle and induced tranquillity at any time.

The Tea Ceremony, it has been said, 'is a subject upon which Japanese and foreign authors alike have written a great deal that is partial or exaggerated or merely foolish'.[11] In the light of that caveat one may be wise, as in most matters relating to Zen, to restrict description and comment to a bare minimum. But we are on safe ground perhaps if we cite some observations made by Father João Rodrigues (1562–1633), the Portuguese Jesuit, who spent more than 30 years in Japan and in matters pertaining to Japanese language and culture showed an insight seldom attained by a Westerner. Rodrigues points out that everything used in the Tea Ceremony 'is as rustic, rough, completely unrefined and simple as nature made it, after the style of a solitary and rustic hermitage'[12]. The purpose of the Tea Ceremony, he declares, 'is to produce courtesy, politeness, modesty, exterior moderation, calmness, peace of body and soul without

The tea ceremony was an important part of the samurai's spiritual and intellectual recreation. Within its rigid simplicity lay many layers of understanding and enjoyment.
Above left: A tea house in the Gosho Palace gardens in Kyoto, the palace customarily used by retired emperors.
Above: An informal tea house in the grounds of the Katsura Imperial Villa in Kyoto. The gardens were laid out in the early seventeenth century. In typical Japanese style, the interior seems to merge into the garden, and this beautiful building became known as the Shōkin-tei, or Pine-Lute Pavilion because of the sound of the wind in the trees

any pride or arrogance, fleeing from all ostentation, pomp, external grandeur, and magnificence'.[13]

Although the Tea Ceremony became very much part of the warrior's culture where it may be said to have had a softening, civilizing influence, its practice was by no means confined to Zen monks and samurai. Humble folk no less than nobles and warriors were welcome to participate. The Ceremony may be seen as perhaps a singular example of democracy in action during a period when any concept of democracy, as understood in modern times, was utterly alien to Japanese thought. Father Rodrigues, when discussing the Tea Ceremony, refers to the 'naturally melancholy disposition' of the Japanese, and speaks of 'decrepitude' as one feature of the utensils used in the making and drinking of the tea. The comment is perceptive. For the aesthetic quality known in Japanese as *sabi*, which is most profoundly felt in the Tea Ceremony, always implies the taking of pleasure in something that is old, faded, a little rusty, or lonely. There is a related concept, *wabi*; which may be translated, not wholly adequately, as 'a taste for the simple and quiet'. A modern tea master tells us: 'The man who believes implicitly in *wabi* casts away everything that is un-necessary except for those requirements which are essential to practical living. To observers from the outside, his life may seem frugal and miserable, but for the true adherent it is the attainment of a peaceful frame of mind in the transience of the temporal world.'[14]

The Tea Ceremony, then, brought the samurai into a quietist dimension wholly removed from the exigencies of combat or of training and practice in the martial arts. His swords left outside, the samurai entered the tea-hut through a low door, virtually doubling his body in order to do so. With other guests he would sit motionless and in silence, watching the faint wisp of smoke from an incense stick, and the steam rising from the kettle, until the moment when the bowl was placed before him. Then, lifting it with both hands, feeling its warmth and texture, he would drink from the bowl in three sips, the last of which, according to etiquette, should be both deep and audible.

The standards of taste, summed up by *wabi*, set by the Tea Ceremony exerted a lasting influence on the style of living adopted not only by the samurai but also by the people at large. The austere design and furnishing of the fifteenth-century tea-hut or tea-room created what in the twentieth century has come to be regarded as the traditional Japanese interior. Gardens, flower arrangement, and the potter's art were to record the same strong influence.

It would be a mistake, needless to say, to imagine that flamboyance, emotional excess, and extravagances of colour and decoration ranging from the attractively ingenious to the merely vulgar, were banished from samurai society during the turbulent years of the fifteenth and sixteenth centuries. In the first place, that society was far from static. Notably in the sixteenth century there was the phenomenon of *gekokujō* ('those below overthrow those above'), meaning upheavals at all levels—peasants rebelling against landlords as well as vassals dispossessing their lords. The parvenu and the turncoat—terms that in practice were very often synonymous—were to be found among many of the warrior captains who overthrew established territorial magnates and became in their turn *sengoku daimyō*, 'civil war barons'. Whatever their valour on the battlefield, such men were not necessarily immune to the seduction of conspicuous expenditure and display. The two most famous *sengoku daimyō*, Oda Nobunaga (1534–82) and Toyotomi Hideyoshi (1536–98), set an example in the construction and decoration of their castles that was decidedly ostentatious—though at the same time it was heroic, and therefore impressive rather than vulgar, at least by European standards.

Secondly, the Muromachi Bakufu, which was extinguished by Nobunaga in 1573, had thrown up two shoguns—Yoshimitsu (1358–1408) and Yoshimasa (1445–90)—who gave themselves over to many lavish and superbly refined forms of aesthetic indulgence. Yoshimitsu's Kyoto palace, the Hana-no-Gosho, was a grand structure set in a garden filled with a profusion of flowers. Indeed he had a passion for novelties of every kind, and also for the niceties of court etiquette. It was under the patronage of Yoshimitsu, moreover, that the Noh drama was developed and refined, as a supreme expression of what is implied by the term, *yūgen* meaning 'subtle profundity', or 'remote and mysterious', something not to be easily expressed in words. The masks worn in Noh by those acting the parts of women or supernatural beings achieved perfection during this period. 'So subtle was the carving that even in one mask worn throughout a performance a shift in the tilt of the head produced a change of expression'[15] Encouraged by Yoshimitsu, there flourished not only new and deeply moving performances of Noh but also a critical, expository, literature on Noh that set standards to which all later generations of actors aspired.

We see here a repetition of what had happened two centuries earlier, when the Taira fell under the spell of the court and capital. The warrior, sometimes despite himself, tends to acquire the attitudes of the court noble. It is not surprising that when the last Bakufu was established, under the Tokugawa house in the early seventeenth century, its location

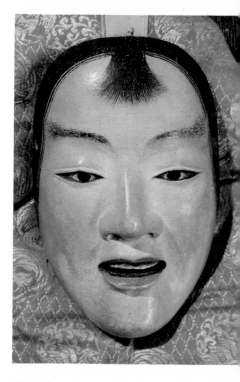

Noh drama was developed during the Muromachi Bakufu, another sign of its burgeoning culture. It was to become the accepted form of dignified theatre suitable for the cultured samurai, as opposed to the more sensational Bunraku and Kabuki forms.

Above: This Noh mask attributed to Echi, dated 1370, is of a young monk. It achieves an expressive power while relying on the minimum of detail.

Right: A mask dated 1390 depicting a samurai; samurai legends played an important part in Noh drama.

Above right: A screen depicting a more popular type of performance taking place at Shijō-gawa, Kyoto, in the late Muromachi period. Kabuki was to develop from this type of theatre

was in the East, in the historic home ground of the samurai order, far from the dangerous, and ultimately enervating, attractions of Kyoto.

In this book, we cannot dwell on the subject, fascinating and instructive as it is, of Muromachi art and culture. It need only be said that Chinese influence was marked and persistent, but was well assimilated, like so many earlier and later importations from abroad, and in the end became very much part of the whole Japanese tradition.

Into this world of brutality and good taste, of Spartan ethics and Athenian sensibility, there intruded in the sixteenth century high-pooped carracks from the Tagus, bearing Christian priests and merchants. Of immediate interest to the samurai was a new weapon which the Portuguese brought with them: namely, the arquebus, the smooth-bore musket. These were soon being fashioned by the Japanese, and the gunsmith's art was to spread to regions that had never seen a Portuguese. But the musket, useful as it was, never acquired the prestige of the sword —perhaps because firearms may have retained the taint of being 'foreign'. As a weapon it was more or less confined to the *ashigaru,* the foot-soldier of a rank at the bottom of the samurai hierarchy.

Yet it was from the category of the *ashigaru* that there emerged one of the great dictatorial figures of Japanese history: Toyotomi Hideyoshi. Two of Hideyoshi's major undertakings, when he had become master of the country, are pertinent to a study of the samurai. The first is his Sword

Hunt; the second is the expedition he dispatched to Korea with the intention of conquering the Chinese empire.

In 1588 Hideyoshi issued an edict, the relevant sections of which read: 'The people of the various provinces are strictly forbidden to have in their possession any swords, short swords, bows, spears, firearms, or other types of arms. The possession of unnecessary implements (of war) makes difficult the collection of taxes and dues and tends to foment uprisings . . . Therefore the heads of provinces, official agents, and deputies are ordered to collect all the weapons mentioned above and turn them over to the government.

'Swords and short swords thus collected will not be wasted. They shall be used as nails and bolts in the construction of the Great Image of Buddha. This will benefit the people not only in this life but also in the next . . .

'In other lands, such as China, the ruler Yao converted rare swords and sharp weapons into agricultural implements after he had established peace. In our country such an experiment has never been made. Thus, all the people should . . . give their undivided attention to agriculture and sericulture.

'All implements mentioned above shall be collected and submitted forthwith.'[16]

It need hardly be said that 'the people of the various provinces' to whom the edict applied did not include those recognized as samurai. But the edict did affect a growing number of farmers who had access to weapons and who from time to time took part in violent uprisings, sometimes led by minor gentry of the samurai order, against the national or local government, or against landlords or moneylenders. The Sword Hunt, it seems, was a success. Together with a compulsory census and registration of all who worked on the land, it achieved its object—the immobilization, no less than the disarmament, of the farmers, who

Hideyoshi's official buildings were often deliberately ostentatious.
Left: The keep or tenshu-kaku, *literally 'the heavenly protector's high structure', of Himeji Castle— largely rebuilt by Hideyoshi.*
Above: The brilliant interior of Hideyoshi's audience chamber, formerly in his Fushimi Castle and now part of a Kyoto temple

57

constituted the great majority of the population. Above all, the Swor
Hunt had the effect of establishing a rigid and more or less permanen
division between the samurai and the rest of society. To a great exten
of course, this division existed already. But the boundary lines betwee
one class and another, though distinct, could be crossed, especially durin
the civil wars of the Muromachi period. Hideyoshi's edict foreshadowe
the further crystallization of the main social classes under the Tokugaw
regime in the seventeenth century. The edict clearly reveals the commo
attitude of the samurai towards the farmers—the tiresome but indis
pensable masses who should be humoured or bullied into accepting thei
lot. The farmer was to stay in his village, work hard, pay his dues, an
leave all political and military affairs to his betters.

During the long Tokugawa peace, which began in the seventeent
century and ended in the nineteenth, certain respectable persons outsid
the samurai class were permitted to bear swords as an honourable badg
of their status. Such men included headmen of important villages and
number of petty officials on the borderline of samurai rank. But the

carried a single sword. The samurai alone had the privilege of bearing two swords, the long *(tachi)* and the short *(wakizashi)*.

Little need be said about Hideyoshi's ambitious venture on the continent, launched in the late spring of 1592. Its purpose was nothing less than the conquest of China by invasion through Korea. The huge army dispatched by Hideyoshi—who himself never left Japan—numbered more than 200,000. There now occurred the first battles between a samurai host and a foreign army for more than 300 years. At first things went well for the Japanese, and one division fought its way north to reach Seoul within three weeks of landing in Korea. But the tide turned when the Chinese intervened, crossing the Yalu and forcing the invaders to retreat. There ensued a struggle that lasted intermittently for about six years, until Hideyoshi's death in 1598 provided an opportunity for the withdrawal of the whole force from Korea.

There can be no doubt that a prime consideration behind the entire venture—although it may have weighed in Hideyoshi's mind less than his ambition to make the Emperor of Japan the ruler of China—was to provide the samurai, and in particular the *daimyō* (the great lords), with an outlet for their fighting energies. Civil war at home had only recently ceased. Psychologically, the samurai were in no mood to contemplate a period of prolonged peace. It was only prudent to let them rampage on foreign soil.

It is no doubt hazardous to generalize about samurai behaviour in Korea; after all, something like a quarter of a million warriors crossed the Tsushima Strait from Japan. But it is a fact that their presence in Korea left a legacy of hatred that still smouldered three centuries later. The fighting did not eliminate many of the restive daimyo, but among their retainers the losses were very high. It may not be wholly fanciful to suppose that at least some of the bellicose passion endemic, so it seems, in sixteenth century Japan burned itself out during the rigours of the savage warfare in Korea. But the only verifiable gain from this whole adventure seems to have been the consignment of 76,000 pickled ears sliced off the 38,000 heads said to have been taken from slain Koreans and Chinese during the last months of the war. These trophies found a resting place in the Mimizuka, or Ear Tomb, in Kyoto.

Among the leading commanders in Korea was the daimyo, Konishi Yukinaga, while another of equal eminence was the daimyo, Kato Kiyomasa. A most unfriendly rivalry existed between them. Kato detested Konishi; and it was *odium theologicum* that divided them. Kato Kiyomasa was a fanatical adherent of the Nichiren sect of Buddhism, perhaps the most explicitly nationalist, pugnaciously ethnocentric faith that has ever sheltered under the canopy of the Mahayana doctrine. He hated Konishi above all because the latter was a Christian.

In this matter, however, Konishi Yukinaga was no eccentric figure, at least in his own region of Japan, which was Kyushu. Nearly 50 years had passed since the Spanish Jesuit, Francis Xavier, had landed at Kagoshima. Since then Catholic Christianity had gained converts running into scores of thousands. In the beginning, at all events, the alien faith won the allegiance of at least a substantial part of samurai society in Kyushu.

Why was this so? It seems surprising that Japanese warriors, inheritors of Shinto, reared in Confucianism, attached to one or other sect of Buddhism, influenced in greater or less degree by Zen, should have been drawn to the Christian doctrine. The answer is almost certainly to be found in the character and personality of the Iberian, particularly Portuguese, missionaries. The ablest of these were the Jesuits. They belonged to a newly established religious order, an intellectual *élite*, the spearhead of the Counter Reformation. They had had the political nous to realize that the conversion of the samurai class, and if possible the daimyo to whom the samurai owed loyalty, was the only really effective way to spread the Gospel in Japan. Accordingly, the Jesuit Fathers

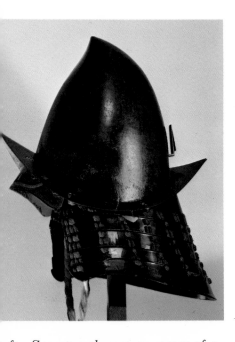

Left: Seventeenth-century screen of a Portuguese carrack lying to off Nagasaki. The samurai official in the foreground, with his long sword lying before him on the ground and his short sword sheathed in his belt, is smoking tobacco—introduced to Japan by Europeans. The Goanese members of the crew have obviously intrigued the artist even more than the Portuguese.

Above: European armour was often used by the Japanese, or, as in this case, copied. This samurai helmet was made by Saotome Ietada in 1600 and is modelled entirely on a European type

applied themselves to a study of the language and customs of the samurai. The samurai for their part, curious and in many cases well-disposed (for the Portuguese traders brought in muskets, tobacco, and other novelties), watched the missionaries with great attention. It only needed a show of geniality towards the strangers by an important lord to start what may have been at first a fashionable dalliance, but which might later develop into a commitment that could lead to a martyr's death.

As might be expected, once a samurai sincerely accepted the new faith his allegiance was staunch. In fact Zen may have played a part in this, because it tended to separate the individual from any institutional religious attachments. Zen could lead to moral anarchy. As one commentator puts it: 'where the mind, inflated by a so-called "cosmic consciousness", is supported only by an ethic based on untutored natural instincts, the results, in terms of wilful and even arrogant conduct, can easily be predicted.'[17] It is at least possible that those ineffable Zen concepts of 'no-mind', 'void', 'emptiness', left the soul of the samurai unsatisfied, depending of course on the nature and disposition of each individual. What can be said with greater assurance is that for the samurai, strongly drawn to the Tea Ceremony, the service of the Mass would present some familiar features.

However, the impact of Christianity on samurai society, which was of some importance at the time and is of perennial interest for the modern scholar, left no visible lasting impression. A hundred years after Xavier every sign of Christianity in Japan appeared to have been stamped out. Materially at any rate Catholic Christianity, it can be said, influenced the course of Japanese life only in the negative sense of stimulating a determined reaction against European contacts in general. Historians have had sharp disagreements about the role of the Portuguese and Spanish missionaries in Japan. Some have argued that the Japanese had every right to be suspicious of the foreigners, in view of what had happened in Mexico, Peru and the Philippines. Thus expulsion was logical, even necessary; ruthless persecution was inevitable, and its methods were no more cruel than those often used in Europe at that time. Others have contended that, despite some instances of tactless speech and behaviour, the foreign missionaries displayed on the whole a great sensitivity *vis à vis* the psychology of the Japanese ruling class. Therefore, the expulsion of foreigners, the closing of the country, and the savage suppression of Christianity were unnecessary, were indicative of something approaching paranoia, and seriously distorted and harmed the development of the Japanese nation. It is certainly piquant to speculate on what might have occurred if the Tokugawa shogunate had not imposed a policy of isolation and had tolerated the missionary activities of foreign and native priests. No doubt Christian samurai would have carried the sword and the Cross to the Melanesians and Maoris.

In the event, Japan closed its doors and settled down to a long period of comparative domestic peace and order. In those years of late feudalism the samurai, while remaining a warrior, was seen to be above all a member of a self-perpetuating bureaucracy, wielding the pen (or, more accurately, the brush) rather than the sword. The samurai becomes, in other words, the armed mandarin.

Right: The Ginkaku-ji represents the surrender of the Muromachi warrior to the aestheticism of Kyoto. The retired Shogun Yoshimasa lived here, and, as one old-fashioned guide book has unkindly expressed it, was surrounded by 'court dames, bepowdered poetasters, actors and libertines who abetted him in his caprices . . .'

60

THE ARMED MANDARINS
Samurai in the Tokugawa period

The long peace of the Tokugawa age was born of conflict, of which the last spasms were the Battle of Sekigahara in 1600 and the Siege of Osaka in 1614–15. Sekigahara established Tokugawa supremacy; Osaka confirmed it. These military episodes provide notable examples of commendable as well as repellent samurai conduct in battle; and they constitute the last instances of full-scale civil war (if we exclude the costly but local Shimabara rising of Christians in 1637) until the break-up of the shogunate in the second half of the nineteenth century.

Before the self-made dictator, Toyotomi Hideyoshi, died in 1598 at the age of 62 it was his great hope and desire that his son, Hideyori, should succeed him as ruler of Japan in the Emperor's name. But the boy was only five years old when Hideyoshi was stricken with his last illness, so elaborate arrangements had to be made for the guardianship of Hideyori until the child should come of age. The guardians, who swore to remain loyal to the house of Toyotomi, came from among the most powerful barons, of whom the leading figure was Tokugawa Ieyasu, daimyo of the Kantō region.

Once Hideyoshi was dead, however, the council of guardians did not long maintain their unity. A serious rift opened between two rival groups, formed to some extent along geographical lines. Ieyasu, supported mainly by the lords of eastern Japan, was opposed by Ishida Mitsunari and a number of daimyo from the west. The animosities that disrupted the

Left : Nijō Castle, the Kyoto headquarters of the Tokugawa Bakufu. Despite its appearance, this is not a fortress but a richly decorated palace

63

Right : The Karamon gate of Nijō Castle is believed to have been taken from Hideyoshi's castle at Momoyama. The elaborate workmanship is typical of late sixteenth-century taste. Nijō Castle was extensively renovated by Tokugawa Ieyasu to serve as the shogun's residence on visits to Kyoto. Far right : The siege of Osaka Castle, shown on a screen commissioned from an unknown artist by Kuroda Nagamasa (1568–1623), a general who took part in the siege. This crucial battle consolidated Tokugawa power. Ieyasu's victory was completed during the second siege called the 'Summer Campaign'

guardians and gave rise to the opposing combinations of warriors soor exploded into open warfare. In October, 1600, this reached its climax ir the great Battle of Sekigahara in central Japan near Gifu. The armies o the west were overwhelmingly defeated, even though they occupied strong position and outnumbered the forces of Ieyasu. But Ieyasu wa something of a military genius; he had earlier arranged, with characteristi cunning and forethought, for a leading enemy general to change sides at crucial moment in the fight, and so he could be confident of victory fror the start.

In the rout that ensued Ishida Mitsunari was captured. He did no it seems, regard this as an intolerable disgrace; for he told Ieyasu's sta that he could easily have killed himself but thought it better to give hi enemies the trouble of putting an end to him. Another importan prisoner was Konishi Yukinaga, the Christian general who had achieve fame in the invasion of Korea. When captured he was invited to comm suicide, but he declined to do so, since this would be a sin according t the law of his Church. So both Ishida and Konishi were exhibited, wit placards round their necks declaring them to be disturbers of the peac to the populace of Osaka and Sakai. They were then beheaded by th Kamo River in Kyoto. On the way to execution Ishida stopped and aske for a cup of tea. Somebody offered him a persimmon. He refused i saying it would upset his digestion.

'It hardly seems necessary', observed Konishi, 'to consider one digestion just before decapitation.'

'That shows how little you understand', Ishida replied: 'You can neve tell how things will turn out the next minute, and so while you hav breath in your body you have got to take care of yourself.'[1]

At Sekigahara the most important weapon seems to have been th musket, followed by the spear and the bow. Every samurai took a swor into battle, in addition to his main weapon, which might be a musket spear, or bow. But in the clash of arms at the height of the battle th sword played a secondary role.

In the vanquished forces of the west there were 87 daimyo. All bu six lost their life or their domain or their freedom. The victoriou Ieyasu rearranged the daimyo map of Japan into a pattern designed t perpetuate the hegemony of his family. Thus the two classes of territoria lord, the *Fudai* and *Tozama daimyō* were established. The former wer those whom Ieyasu considered loyal and reliable; they had either fough

64

on his side at Sekigahara or had helped him in other ways. The *Tozama* lords, on the other hand, were those who had opposed him in battle or else had hesitated to pledge allegiance pending the outcome of the campaign. Notable among the *Tozama daimyō* was Shimazu of Satsuma, who fought on the wrong side but managed to evade capture after Sekigahara and contrived to return safely home to Kyushu. He was too powerful to be removed from his fief. There were certain other lords whom Ieyasu thought it imprudent to oppress, and they too were classed as *Tozama*.

Sekigahara has always been regarded as a watershed in Japanese history. Yet it seems clear that Ieyasu could not feel wholly at ease after his victory; for many barons, including every *Tozama daimyō*, cherished warm memories of Hideyoshi and therefore centred their affections and hopes on the young Hideyori. Three years after Sekigahara, Ieyasu secured for himself the office of shogun. In accordance with a tradition established in the Kamakura period, this office was confined to members of the house of Minamoto, to which Ieyasu belonged. In 1605 he handed over the shogunate to his son Hidetada, but retirement, as has often been the case throughout Japanese history, meant very little. Ieyasu was now 63, with a lifetime of military campaigns and political manoeuvres behind him, but he had little thought of relaxing his grip on the levers of power. The transfer of title to his son was advantageous in that it relieved Ieyasu

of any purely ceremonial duties he might wish to avoid, while it no doubt helped to consolidate his new shogunal line.

There remained the problem of Hideyori and the house of Toyotomi to which Ieyasu was constrained to profess not only goodwill but also vague deference. Hideyori was still only a boy when he was given Ieyasu' grand-daughter in marriage. He retained a substantial domain in the provinces close to Osaka where he lived with his mother and a band of retainers in Osaka castle, the vast fortress completed by Hideyoshi in 1590. The tension existing between Osaka and the Tokugawa shogunate based on Yedo (the modern Tokyo), is illustrated by the fact that his mother would not allow Hideyori to accept a pressing invitation to visit Yedo. She announced that she would kill him rather than let him make the journey.

In 1614, however, after he had completed his military preparations, Ieyasu picked a quarrel with Hideyori and proceeded to besiege Osaka

*etails from the screen depicting the
ge of Osaka which is also shown
page 65.*

*elow: The civilian population flee
e overrun castle as Hideyori's
use is lost.*

*elow right: A ferocious clash of
ms – the horned helmet indicates
e figure of Honda Tadatomo, one of
yasu's captains, as he leads an
tack on the Osaka defenders. Also
this detail is the figure of a
murai with an arquebus raised to
s shoulder, but firearms were used
little effect in this battle*

castle with an army not far short of 100,000 warriors. Well before this final breach with Hideyori, Ieyasu had obtained cannon and ammunition, from the English East India Company, which for some ten years maintained a trading post at Hirado in Kyushu. These were intended for use specifically in the Osaka operation.

The outer wall and moat at Osaka had a circumference of just under nine miles (14 km). They enclosed a second moat and wall, and behind these was a network of watch-towers and redoubts protecting the heart of the fortress, the *hon-maru* ('centre circle') from which rose the high white keep with its fluted tiles and curving eaves.

To defend this stronghold there mustered in support of Hideyori and his mother, Yodogimi, an enormous force, estimated at some 90,000, made up very largely of *rōnin* from all over Japan. A *rōnin* (literally 'wave man') was a masterless samurai. This category had long existed, but it was much enlarged in the aftermath of Sekigahara, when so many fiefs

were confiscated and reallocated by the victorious Ieyasu. In the literature and folklore of the samurai the ronin plays a colourful role. At his best he is a sort of knight-errant, ready to place his sword at the service of the oppressed, alert for any act of daring, caring nothing for his own safety but only for the call of honour and the stimulus of adventure. At his worst the ronin is a swashbuckling bully and rogue; for authority a tiresome disturber of the peace, and for the common people a dangerous nuisance to be avoided or, if necessary, temporarily placated. In what proportions these contrasting types were represented at Osaka it is of course impossible to guess. Judging, however, from the fighting spirit displayed during the struggle one may say at least that the ronin warriors defending the castle can have included few craven souls.

The *châtelaine*, Yodogimi, had been Hideyoshi's favourite mistress. She was the daughter of a prominent *sengoku daimyō* (Asai Nagamasa) who had committed suicide while she was still a small child after defeat in battle. Her mother, who was a noted beauty, married again, but her second husband met his death fighting against Hideyoshi. Yodogimi's mother, widowed for the second time, took her own life rather than escape or face the risk of capture.

When the siege of Osaka began in November 1614 Yodogimi was 47 years of age, but, true to her martial inheritance, she was a commanding figure. She was clad in armour when she inspected the defences, thereby stiffening the resolve of the garrison, although the comment has been made, rather unkindly, that 'the soldiers seem to have regarded this

In peace and war there was often
great mistrust between rival daimyo.
Spies and counterspies were used,
mostly drawn from samurai initiates
in ninjutsu, 'the martial art of
invisibility', who were known as
ninja.
Above: An Ukiyo-e, *or Tokugawa
period popular print, of a ninja
making secret finger signs.*
*Right: Interior of a house as used by
a ninja, with secret storage places for
weapons under the raised floor.*
Far right: Wall painting of a
tengu, *a winged, long-nosed goblin,
painted in about 1800. In the
esoteric mythology of the* ninja *a*
tengu *is a patron spirit*

demonstration with mixed feelings, and rather as a suggestion that they were hard up for leaders'.[2]

Ieyasu, who was now over 70, directed operations mainly from his headquarters in the field, a simple hut, rather like a tea-room, which he had built on a hillock facing the castle. But this veteran of nearly 90 battles (he had fought his first at the age of 17) did not forget his own precept: that a general does not win by contemplating the backs of his men's necks. So on many occasions he joined his son, the shogun Hidetada, in reconnoitring the castle from the front line.

Prolonged assaults in icy weather through the first winter months brought no success to the besieging armies. On the contrary, they suffered heavy losses, estimated according to some accounts to have been as high as 30,000. So Ieyasu had recourse to intrigue. He made proposals for peace that were unwisely accepted by Hideyori on the advice of Yodogimi. At first sight the terms proposed may not have seemed unreasonable. Hideyori was to retain possession of the castle and his domains, and no penalties were to be visited on any ronin who left Osaka and returned home. However, it was stipulated also that at least the greater part of the outer moat should be filled in by the Tokugawa forces, at their expense.

When these terms were accepted Ieyasu directed Honda Masazumi, one of his subordinates, to undertake the filling in of the moat. The order was obeyed with alacrity. Not only was the moat filled in but the outer wall was demolished at the same time. Moreover, Honda's men began filling in the second moat and even made a start on pulling down the second wall. The Osaka leaders naturally protested: but they had difficulty in finding Honda, who was absent due to 'ill health'. The matter had to be handled by correspondence; until at last Honda admitted that he had misunderstood, and therefore exceeded, his orders. So the demolition work was called off. But by this time the outer defences of the castle had been destroyed. When Hideyori's complaints reached Ieyasu that old badger is reported to have sent his apologies and to have indicated that he would condemn Honda to death, but for the fact that such an action would mar the harmony of the newly established peace. 'Fortunately', said Ieyasu, 'peace has now been concluded. Let us not talk any more about the castle's moats and ramparts'.

So ended the first, abortive, attack on Osaka castle. It was known to posterity as 'The Winter Campaign' *(Fuyu no Jin)*, a phrase that passed into samurai language as epitomizing the folly committed when the strong undermine their own position by yielding to the promptings of pacifist feeling.

69

When, as was inevitable, hostilities were resumed, in the late spring of 615, the fighting was at first indecisive. Indeed there were moments when it looked as though the Tokugawa host might be driven off in confusion and disarray. Hideyori's ronin, no longer able to rely on purely defensive tactics, did most of the fighting outside the walls. These sallies were costly, but nearly succeeded. When they ultimately failed, however, the besieged garrison had only half-filled moats and half-demolished walls to fall back on. When the retreat occurred, after many days of desperate hand-to-hand clashes, the end came quickly. Ieyasu's men fought their way into the inner defence zone. It is said that the chief cook at Osaka was bribed by Ieyasu to set fire to the kitchen. Be that as it may, the fire that broke out in the keep, was ignited by someone in the garrison. Another possibility is that the fire was the work of a spy versed in *ninjutsu*, 'the martial art of invisibility'. The practitioners of this esoteric art, who were known as *ninja*, guarded their secrets so well that little is known of them even today. But as assassins, 'cat burglars', and special agents they played an active though stealthy part in most of the wars, plots, and counter-plots of the feudal age.

During the final hours Hideyori's wife, Ieyasu's grand-daughter, sent a message to the Tokugawa camp, begging Ieyasu to spare the lives of her husband and her mother-in-law, Yodogimi. Ieyasu was unmoved by his appeal, although he gave orders that his grand-daughter herself must not be killed. As the inner fortress fell, Hideyori committed suicide and Yodogimi was killed by one of his retainers to save her from being captured.

It was claimed that enemy heads counted after Sekigahara numbered about 35,000. The figure for the Osaka 'Summer Campaign' (*Natsu no Jin*) cannot have been less. At least one highway into Kyoto became an avenue of heads which had been placed on rows of planks as far as the eye could see.

Determined to liquidate all who might in future cause trouble to his descendants, Ieyasu sought out Hideyori's illegitimate son, a child of six called Kunimatsu. He had the boy beheaded by a common executioner in Kyoto. Such inhumanity broke all the conventions of the time; but it cannot be doubted that Ieyasu remembered the evil consequences for the Taira of the mercy shown by Kiyomori to Yoritomo and Yoshitsune.

The account of the Winter and Summer Campaigns makes it clear that it was only after the fall of Osaka that the new regime was really secure. One is inclined to agree with the view, even if it rather overstates the case, that 'Sekigahara was merely a prelude to Osaka . . . the former stood to the latter almost in the relation of a preliminary skirmish'.[3]

There was treachery at both Sekigahara and Osaka. But the loyalty of the ronin at Osaka exhibited a particular facet of some interest, for the Osaka warriors were inspired by the memory of a man who had been dead for nearly 20 years—Toyotomi Hideyoshi. His son, and Yodogimi, were of course living symbols to keep the memory green: and round Hideyori there accrued after the fall of Osaka the body of myth that sometimes attaches itself to a young hero whose death cannot easily be accepted. There were stories that he had escaped and was hiding in Kyushu. Somewhat similar legends had grown up round Yoshitsune and had persisted long after his *seppuku*. It was, above all, the force of nostalgia that brought ronin swarming to the defence of Osaka in the hope of seeing once again the Toyotomi banner with the gourd crest victorious against all foes. Thus in the flames and gun-smoke of Osaka there ended for ever the bloody pageant of embattled samurai armies—scores of thousands of warriors—that had characterized so much of Japanese history for nearly 500 years.

There followed—and it was a process that occupied many years—what can only be called the taming of the samurai. This does not mean, needless to say, that the warrior was encouraged to forget his martial skills. The tiger's claws were sheathed, but they must be kept in good

After his death, Ieyasu, founder of the Tokugawa Bakufu, was deified as an incarnation of the Buddha. His grandson, the shogun Iemitsu, decided to build a mausoleum suitable for his venerated grandfather. He selected the site of Nikko and also had his own mausoleum, the Daiyuin, erected there.
Left : One of the two guardian divinities that protect the entrance gate of the Daiyuin. Usually represented as muscular giants, the Niō, as they are called, are of Indian provenance and are often found on guard at the entrance to Buddhist temples.
Above : The drumtower of the Daiyuin

condition. Nevertheless as the decades passed without the call to arms, these great cats became almost domesticated, though they always retained the deference of the commoners who made up about 90 per cent of the population. Some of the commoners might wax fat and even put on airs, particularly among the merchant class, but they did not aspire to challenge their betters; they knew that the samurai remained dangerous creatures, ready to pounce at the slightest hint of insolence or disrespect.

The Tokugawa shogunate, based on the castle at Yedo, was to maintain its power, preserving domestic peace in spite of occasional disturbances of a local character, until the arrival in strength of the Western powers in the 1850s. The Tokugawa system, it has been truly remarked, 'had no ready counterpart in the national structures of other societies' and 'must be understood in its own terms as a political organism in which the daimyo set the basic pattern of local government, accepting a unity under the shogun which precluded further warfare but which left them a considerable degree of autonomy.'[4]

A prime means of maintaining that 'unity under the shogun' was the system known as *sankin kōtai* or 'alternate attendance', whereby the territorial lords, great and small, were required to spend a regular portion

of their time in attendance at the shogun's castle and to leave their wives and families in Yedo when they returned to their own domains. This custom was not invented by Ieyasu and his descendants. It had been enforced to some extent by the Kamakura Bakufu, and Hideyoshi, too, had compelled provincial lords to attend on him at Osaka castle and had made them leave their wives and children in Osaka when they visited their fiefs. But under the Tokugawa regime the system was established on a permanent basis.

Every daimyo, then, had a town house in Yedo; and in most cases this was the only home his wife and children knew. Great care was taken by the Bakufu to ensure that it had reliable knowledge of samurai movements into and out of the city. Barriers on the roads out of Yedo were manned by guards ordered to watch for 'women going out and guns coming in', since anyone thinking of rebellion would try to get his family out while smuggling weapons in.

The mausoleums at Nikko have been criticized for the garishness of their architecture, but they are beautifully set among a forest of cryptomeria. Iemitsu's motive for building them may not only have been prestige – by accumulating the resources necessary for the project, he also concentrated wealth in the hands of the shogunate.
Above left: A simple well in the grounds of Nikko.
Above: Nikko was intended as a centre of pilgrimage – an equivalent to Ise – in order to give permanent legitimacy to the Yedo Bakufu

Thus the roads leading to Yedo saw a more or less constant movement of samurai attending their daimyo on his visits to and from the Tokugawa capital. The obligation of *sankin kōtai* affected well over 200 daimyo, and the warrior processions to and from Yedo were a favourite subject for artists of the woodblock print. One can visualize the scene rather clearly: the retinue of pike-men, musketeers, grooms and porters walking before and behind the lacquered split-bamboo palanquin carrying the daimyo himself, with the leaders of the procession shouting in compelling and rebarbative tones the Japanese equivalent of: 'Bow! Bow! Ye Tradesmen and Ye Masses!'

Pageantry and display were important features of such processions; and as the harsh imperatives of the battlefield faded from memory the spears, guns, bows and arrows began to assume a role that was primarily symbolic and ornamental. As for the numbers involved, these varied according to the rank of each provincial baron. Kaempfer, a German physician with the Dutch East India Company at Nagasaki, travelled to Yedo in 1692. He records, though perhaps with some exaggeration, that the procession of 'one of the chief Daimios' filled up the road 'for some days' and amounted 'to about 20,000 men more or less'.[5]

In one domain, namely Sendai in the north-east, the *sankin kōtai* system was reproduced on a small scale. That is to say, many vassals of Date, the *Tozama daimyō* of Sendai, lived in their own localities but were required to reside at Sendai for fixed periods. In nearly all the other domains this kind of arrangement was unknown: it was unnecessary because the territorial lord normally kept his vassals, high and low, permanently resident in his castle town. Another important exception, however, was Satsuma, in Kyushu, where the leading vassals tended to be semi-independent local warriors administering their own districts, with authority over lesser samurai who were as often as not almost indistinguishable, except for their two swords, from the farmers among whom they worked.

The richest daimyo was Maeda, lord of Kaga, on the Japan Sea. His income, based on the assessed productive capacity of the rice crop in his domain, was second only to that of the Bakufu itself. The Maeda house was justly proud of its close links with Ieyasu, for the latter married off his grand-daughter to a Maeda lord; and at Sekigahara the Maeda daimyo had been an ally almost on equal terms with Ieyasu himself. Kanazawa was the capital of the Kaga domain, and here the Maeda, when not in Yedo, resided in their massive castle.

Typically, the provincial castle town was the headquarters of the daimyo; and in and around the castle dwelt the samurai of the domain. In the town outside the castle walls lived the artisans and merchants. In the countryside beyond the town were the farmers or fishermen, and these primary producers were left more or less on their own to administer themselves, provided they met their tax and corvée obligations and kept the peace. In one of his books, Lafcadio Hearn tells us that in the Matsue district of western Japan the records showed that in the villages of the area there had been no crime, even of a petty nature, for many generations. This is more believable than it might seem. The Tokugawa shogunate, it has been claimed, 'was built upon a secure foundation of self-governing hamlets composed of well-disciplined peasants'.[6]

The 'well-disciplined peasants' came second in the hierarchy of the four classes which comprised, in descending order of official importance, the samurai, farmers, artisans and merchants. The Kyoto court nobility (including of course members of the imperial family), the priesthood, and doctors were outside this class structure. So were actors, courtesans, and members of the Eta, or outcaste community. Of a total population that by the end of the seventeenth century may have amounted to about 30,000,000, the samurai numbered probably rather less than 2,000,000. But in the provincial capitals, the castle towns, the samurai often constituted 50 per cent or more of the population. In theory, class barriers were rigid. In practice, there was a good deal of mobility between the lower three classes. But between these and the samurai order of all grades the barrier was usually—though not invariably—insurmountable. Indicative of the general view was the common saying: 'a horse goes with a horse, an ox with an ox.'

The Bakufu went to extraordinary lengths in a ceaseless endeavour to regulate, by sumptuary laws, the behaviour, dress and living conditions of the four social classes. In particular, repeated efforts were made to discourage ostentation and extravagance on the part of the merchants. These efforts often proved unsuccessful. Nothing, it seemed, could prevent the wealthy merchants of Yedo and Osaka from enjoying themselves. Nevertheless, the shogunate endeavoured—except for certain periods when it succumbed itself to the temptations of hedonism—to dragoon the population into following what can only be described as a frugal and puritanical way of life. For it was the firm belief of the samurai

The wealth of the daimyo, assessed on the value of their domainal rice crop, varied greatly. The richest house was that of the Maeda family, lords of Kaga.
Right: The outer ramparts of Kanazawa Castle, the country seat of the head of the Maeda family.
Above: The Myoju-ji at Kanazawa was known as 'The temple of deception'. With the removal of a few boards, a hidden escape route is revealed through which the family could disappear in case of trouble

class that the commonality, unless constantly admonished and checked, was given to a feckless pursuit of self-interest and pleasure.

Tokugawa Ieyasu, in the admonitions he is said to have bequeathed his successors at his death in 1616, declared: 'If fellows of the lower orders go beyond what is proper toward samurai, or if any sub-feudatory samurai is remiss toward a direct retainer, there is no objection to cutting such a one down.'[7] This became known as *kirisute gomen,* or the right 'to cut down and leave'. Since it was a right enjoyed by every grade of warrior, from the daimyo to the roughest foot-soldier, it enforced respect and perpetuated the social and political subordination of the common people. But fear alone, though a factor never to be underestimated, could not have maintained the prestige of the samurai class during the 264 years of the Tokugawa era, from 1603 to 1867. The real basis of that prestige was the warrior's virtual monopoly of moral, political, and intellectual authority, an authority based to a great extent on neo-Confucianism.

Confucianism had always been influential in shaping the ethical code of the samurai class. It was not until the Tokugawa age, however, that this philosophy became the officially approved basis of government and the generally accepted code of all social conduct. There were several schools of Confucian thought, and the one chosen by the Tokugawa Bakufu was the School of neo-Confucianism founded by the Chinese philosopher Chu Hsi (1130–1200). The aim of the Bakufu was: 'to eradicate all thought of insurrection by lower ranking warriors against their lords and . . . to counter the otherworldliness of Buddhism and the teachings of Christianity.'[8]

The foundation of all Confucian schools was the *Analects* of Confucius. The approved attitudes and behaviour patterns stemming from that classic have been listed, by a distinguished American Sinologist, as follows:

1 Submissiveness to authority—parents, elders, and superiors
2 Submissiveness to the mores and the norms
3 Reverence for the past and respect for history
4 Love of traditional learning
5 Esteem for the force of example
6 Primacy of broad moral cultivation over specialized competence
7 Preference for non-violent moral reform in state and society
8 Prudence, caution, preference for a middle course
9 Non-competitiveness
10 Courage and a sense of responsibility for a great tradition
11 Self-respect (with some permissible self-pity) in adversity
12 Exclusiveness and fastidiousness on moral and cultural grounds
13 Punctiliousness in the treatment of others.[9]

These attitudes have been listed specifically in the context of China, but to a considerable degree they faithfully represent ideals of conduct prescribed by the Bakufu, exemplified in theory at least by the samurai

Right: Detail from an early seventeenth-century screen depicting Nijō Castle, the headquarters of the Tokugawa family in Kyoto. Such screens, showing Kyoto and its suburbs, were very popular. A member of the Tokugawa family is leaving the castle to visit the Imperial Palace and is receiving obeisance from the townspeople

class, and accepted by the Japanese population as a whole. It should b
noted, however, that in Tokugawa Japan loyalty to one's lord was mor
important than loyalty to one's parents, a reversal of the Chinese priorities
Had the Chinese pattern been followed in its entirety, with suprem
emphasis placed on loyalty to one's parents, samurai society could not i
the long run have retained its cohesion, and feudalism, as the Japanes
knew it, would have decayed. Even so, Tokugawa encouragement c
Confucian studies, which were decidedly rational and humanist in sub
stance and tone, began to convert the samurai class from a purely militar
oligarchy into a didactic moral and intellectual *élite*. Accordingly, as th
seventeenth century progressed, with the years of peace lengthening int
decades, the warriors of Japan became either bureaucrats following a well
established administrative routine, or janissaries filling in time wit
ceremonial guard duties of a not very demanding nature.

Except in certain *han* (fiefs), such as Satsuma, the samurai had becom
divorced from the land. He lived close to his lord in the castle town—

Yedo, the shogun's capital, was itself the greatest castle town in Japan—and he was paid a regular annual stipend in the form of so many bushels of rice. In other words, he was a strictly non-productive member of society; and, in the absence of domestic warfare and foreign threats or entanglements, his function as a fighting man had disappeared. How was it that in these circumstances he did not become eventually an idle and effete parasite, softened by leisure and corrupted by power?

To a limited extent softening and corruption did occur. At the top of the pyramid, certain shoguns and several daimyo turned out to be entirely decadent: spoilt, feeble-minded, popinjays, debauchees in thrall to concubines or catamites. Ernest Satow, the English scholar-diplomat who acquired first-hand an unrivalled knowledge of the language and society of Japan in the twilight of the feudal age, asserts that the descendants of the great warriors of Ieyasu's time had become 'imbecile puppets'.[10] Lower in the hierarchy, too, there were some signs of deterioration. A samurai was often in debt to a merchant or money-lender. He would be

more or less forced to exchange at least part of his rice stipend for cash; and since it was beneath his dignity to haggle, or even to keep himself accurately informed of the movement of prices, the samurai tended to become indigent, while the merchant grew fat.

Indeed, by the early years of the eighteenth century the self-confidence of the merchants of Yedo and Osaka, although always precarious, attracted much attention, both envious and disapproving. A contemporary observer wrote: 'Nowadays when a samurai writes a letter to a merchant who possesses some wealth, he addresses the latter in the same manner as he would address an exalted personage. When they meet each other on the street and exchange greetings, they both address each other as *dono* ("sire") so that it is difficult to distinguish between the samurai and the merchant. They behave as if they were equals.'[12]

But even supposing the majority of the daimyo to have been by the nineteenth century as feeble and unsatisfactory as Satow suggests, this was a minute fraction of the samurai class. In any case, the personal virtues or defects of a provincial baron, while of some importance for the restricted circle of his *karō* (chief retainers), were not of great moment so far as the attitudes of his other samurai were concerned. Their loyalty was supposed to be, and in most cases during the Tokugawa age must have been, unconditional. The position in many a fief has been described in these terms: 'Despite the nominally absolute and autocratic role of the

In the long peace under the Tokugawa Bakufu, armour was more a symbol of prestige than of warlike intentions. Right : This unusual seventeenth-century suit of armour bears a Buddhist inscription in gold lacquer on the breastplate – the central line reads 'Hail lotus of the good law'. The helmet is in the shape of a folded paper hat. The mask was made in the nineteenth century. Far right : An iron tsuba (sword-guard) made in the eighteenth century. The jumbled characters read : 'A sword which gives life, a blade which kills'. Below : The grotesque profile of a face-mask made by one of the Myōchin family

daimyo, the likelihood of an able individual's inheriting the realm seem to have been rather slight. In fact most able daimyo were adopted son and quite often the top post was all but vacant. The domain of Fukuok: for instance, had virtually no daimyo for a century. With the shogu maintaining the peace, this made no difference in terms of nation: political stability. Nor was the next higher level, of *karō*, limited as it w: to three to five families, much more likely to have the time (considerin residence in Edo) or ability to do very much. Despite nominal authorit at the top, then, each realm found itself with men of considerably low rank, of whom there were far more, having the exercise (though not th recognition) of power.'[12]

Opportunities for responsibility, therefore, enhanced the loyalty t superior authority which the samurai acquired almost before he wa weaned. Indeed, it has been reckoned that the 300 or so fiefs of the lat Tokugawa period made use of an immense samurai bureaucracy.

As for the financial dependence of the samurai on the mercantile com munity, this was not always as baleful as it might seem. It has to b remembered that the status of the merchant was never secure. If h chanced to incur the wrath of the government he could be victimized i exemplary fashion. Proof of great riches was reason enough for the Baku to confiscate a merchant's entire property. It has been suggested that th constant threat prompted leading merchants to lose no time in dissipatir heir accumulated funds in expensive pleasures.[13] This was one reason, doubtless, for the remarkable sophistication and vitality of the Yoshiwara in Yedo, and of other famous entertainment quarters of the great cities.

It seems, then, that despite lapses, the samurai order as a whole preserved its integrity and prestige throughout the Tokugawa age. Its hallmarks during that period were moral restraint, a keen *esprit de corps*, and high regard for intellectual no less than physical excellence. In broad terms, the Tokugawa samurai are like athletes in training for an event that may never take place—athletes, moreover, who while training their muscles are also cultivating their minds.

Zen as a source of strength never dried up, but, as we have seen, from about the middle of the seventeenth century its influence was surpassed by that of Confucianism and its various schools. It may be that the appeal of Zen is strongest when times are turbulent. Certainly the rational, down-to-earth character of Chinese philosophical thought could not fail to diminish the impact of a frankly ineffable faith. Furthermore, for the same reason revealed religion—the many sects of Buddhism—suffered a certain decline in the eyes of the samurai. Yet Shinto did not experience this semi-eclipse. The Sage and his interpreters, greatly revered as they were, could not be permitted to obscure the effulgence of the Ise Shrines.

Now although it may strike the modern scientific intelligence as deplorably narrow and conservative, the Confucian outlook, as a recipe for the harmonious ordering of social life, cannot be described as illogical; and it is not lacking in subtlety or moral worth. The exegesis of the Confucian classics, after all, occupied many of the best minds in Asia, including of course many in Japan.

There was, it must be said, more than a touch of priggishness about the *gravitas* of the typical Tokugawa samurai. Holier-than-thou in his attitude to the vulgar, he was buoyed up, whatever his material circumstances were, by the knowledge that he must always set an example of right conduct. It was, in the final analysis, his adamantine self-esteem that prevented the samurai from lapsing into indolence or venality. It goes without saying that falls from grace were not unknown. For if poverty and debt could drive some samurai, ronin especially, into trade or into home industries such as umbrella-making, printing, brewing, and pottery, the hedonism of city life seduced others into dissipation or crime. Nevertheless, taking the samurai class as a whole, such instances cannot be considered characteristic behaviour.

Within the wide stream of Confucian thought there were, as we have already remarked, many currents. For example, the neo-Confucianism of Chu Hsi, the orthodox doctrine, was challenged, explicitly or by implication, by a number of Japanese scholars. It is well to remember, however, that like the generality of educated men at that time, such challengers would have tended to be eclectic in their views, 'taking the good', as the Japanese put it, 'from many sources'. There were those who propounded the views of Wang Yang-ming (1472–1529), who had attached great importance to intuitive knowledge—representing, in Professor Fairbank's pleasing phrase, 'a sort of Zen revolt within Confucianism'.[14] There were others who claimed that Chu Hsi's teachings distorted true Confucian thought and drew their philosophy directly from the most ancient texts of the Confucian classics.

What is interesting about these and other contending schools is that most of their champions, for all their enthusiasm for Chinese models, could never bring themselves to admit that their own Japanese heritage of beliefs might have to take second place. In one way or another, Confucian ideas were squared with Shinto tradition. So although the samurai of Tokugawa Japan were 'tamed', they were not fully 'civilized' in a sense acceptable to a Chinese mandarin. One difference, of course, between the samurai and a member of the contemporary Ch'ing literati arose from the fact that the Japanese did not adopt the examination system.

Government remained the function of a hereditary class undiluted by talent from below. Had there existed in Japan an examination system of the Chinese type one suspects that as in China the military man sooner or later would have declined in official and popular esteem; and that would have spelt the end of the samurai as the dominant figure in society.

But most of the scholars interested in Chinese ideas were samurai themselves, and so were much concerned to preserve not only the political supremacy of the warrior class but also its martial traditions. The anomalous position of their class in a time of unbroken peace was recognized as a serious problem. It was not enough for the samurai merely to monopolize the bureaucracy of the Bakufu and the domains, even though their position had the support of scriptural authority, since Mencius, the Confucian sage, had said that 'some men use their minds while others use their muscles' and had declared that the second category must be governed by the first. So, as we are told, 'the common people, that is, the peasants, artisans, and the merchants, were permitted to exist only to serve the samurai and to feed the samurai'.[15] But could the iron self-assurance of the samurai have persisted for so long in this hereditary oligarchy without some extra underpinning by foundations even stronger than those provided by the impressive apparatus of classical Chinese ethics and metaphysics?

This extra dimension, which at first supplemented and eventually eclipsed the teachings of the Sage, was the faith in a specifically Japanese 'Way of the Samurai', one translation of this being *bushidō*. A number of scholars and teachers won fame as interpreters of this concept. But none was more influential in the long run—since he may almost be called the inventor of *bushidō*—than Yamaga Sokō (1622–85), a teacher who, among the many schools of Confucianism, followed that of the 'true' or ancient learning *(kōgaku)*. He taught military strategy and tactics as well as the Chinese classics. He was also an historian, though of a kind not free from bias, since he asserted that his native land, being the creation of the gods and blessed by a divine and unbroken line of emperors, surpassed all others and was the true centre of civilization. He delivered a number of attacks on the Chu Hsi school which brought him into disfavour with the shogunate, and he was exiled to the domain of the lord of Akō. This rustication was to have considerable consequences later.

In about the year 1665 the record of lectures given by Yamaga under the title of *Shidō*, 'The Way of the Warrior' was made public. In course of time this became one of the most influential of all moral guides for samurai behaviour. Some passages from it, therefore, should be quoted:

> 'The business of the samurai consists in reflecting on his own station in life, in discharging loyal service to his master if he has one, in deepening his fidelity in association with friends, and, with due consideration of his own position, in devoting himself to duty above all. However, in one's own life, one becomes unavoidably involved in obligations between father and child, older and younger brother, and husband and wife. Though these are also the fundamental moral obligations of everyone in the land, the farmers, artisans, and merchants have no leisure from their occupations, and so they cannot constantly act in accordance with them and fully exemplify the Way. The samurai dispenses with the business of the farmer, artisan, and merchant and confines himself to practising this Way; should there be someone in the three classes of the common people who transgresses against these moral principles, the samurai summarily punishes him and thus upholds proper moral principles in the land. It would not do for the samurai to know the martial and civil virtues without manifesting them. Since this is the case, outwardly he stands in physical readiness for any call to service and inwardly he strives to fulfil the Way of the lord and subject, friend and friend, father and son, older and younger brother, and husband and wife. Within his heart he keeps to the ways of peace, but without he keeps his weapons ready for use. The three classes of the common people make him their teacher and respect him. By following his teachings, they are enabled to understand what is fundamental and what is secondary.
>
> 'Herein lies the Way of the samurai, the means by which he earns his clothing, food, and shelter; and by which his heart is put at ease, and he is enabled to pay back at length his obligations to his lord and the kindness of his parents.'[16]

Nothing, it seems, could be more deeply imbued with the Confucian spirit; and such admonitions illuminate very clearly the moral climate that enveloped and sustained the Tokugawa samurai. 'Within his heart he keeps to the ways of peace, but without he keeps his weapons

Above: Himeji Castle seen through the boughs of cherry trees laden with blossom. Cherry blossom has always been a potent symbol for the samurai. For as the blossom falls at the first puff of wind, so the samurai meets death without hesitation or regret. As the cherry among flowers, so is the bushi (samurai) among men'

ready for use'. That phrase expresses in a nutshell the approved role of the samurai. Notice the primary emphasis given to the relationship of 'lord and subject'—the Japanese adjustment of the Chinese belief that filial piety, the obligation of child to parent, comes first. Observe too the injunction that the samurai should reflect on his own station in life: this is part of 'the business of the samurai'.

Later in his life Yamaga Sokō provided the samurai with additional nourishment; the source here being the never failing spring of national pride. In Yamaga's 'Autobiography in Exile' (*Haisho zampitsu*) he told his readers that although he once thought Japan to be 'inferior in every way to China', he had become aware 'of the serious errors in this view'. Then, after stressing the glory of the imperial line as 'legitimate descendants of the Sun Goddess', Yamaga goes on to praise 'Japan's pursuit

of the way of martial valour'. 'Our valour in war', he says, 'inspired fear in foreigners. As for invasion from abroad, foreigners never conquered us or even occupied or forced cession of our land.'[17] Handed down in warrior households from father to son, these precepts and ideas exerted immense influence, not least in the last years of the Bakufu, when the menace of foreign armed aggression seemed very real.

After Yamaga had fallen foul of the shogunate and had been sent into exile to Akō—in the province of Harima which lies on the northern littoral of the Inland Sea in western Japan—he became a deeply respected teacher in the court of the daimyo, where he spent many years. His influence can be seen in the events concerned in one of the most famous episodes of the Tokugawa period. It was nearly 20 years after Yamaga's death that a grave disaster befell this domain. Its daimyo, the Lord Asano, was ordered while in Yedo to perform *seppuku*. He had committed the unpardonable crime of assaulting a high Bakufu official within the precincts of Yedo Castle.

This was the overture to the celebrated affair of the Akō vendetta, popularly known as the tale of The Forty-seven Ronin. The story illustrates key elements in the samurai code of honour, such as the inescapable obligations of loyalty and revenge, the ruthless suppression of human affections in the service of duty, punctilious regard for etiquette, submission to the lawful authority of the government, and a calm readiness for death by self-immolation. The affair also shows that these qualities, so admirably demonstrated in the consummation of the vendetta, were not very much in fashion when it took place during the first years of the eighteenth century. This was one of the reasons why the drama created such a stir, jolting samurai and townsmen alike into a mood of self-reflection. In fact this period, known from its era name as *Genroku*, has entered the Japanese language as a byword for hedonistic luxury, colour, and extravagance.

The shogun of the day, Tsunayoshi, was a forceful character who exercised absolute power, but certain of his prejudices were so odd as to suggest that his mind was unbalanced. For example, he became known behind his back as 'the Dog Shogun' because of his decree that all animals, but dogs especially, must be treated with the greatest courtesy and consideration. Those responsible for the death of animals or birds had to answer for it, and in certain instances capital punishment was imposed. All the same, his regime coincided with a vigorous effloresence of urban culture, exhibited perhaps more fully by Kyoto and Osaka than Yedo. One has the impression, although it should not be stated too strongly, that in this period the warrior class chose, for the time being, to relax its severely didactic and censorious attitude *vis à vis* the merchant community and its pleasures. Perhaps the capricious, unpredictable character of Tsunayoshi had something to do with this. At all events, it is known, for example, that samurai, albeit usually in some kind of face-saving disguise, defied both custom and sumptuary laws to attend the performances of Bunraku (puppet drama) and Kabuki that were the delight of townsmen. Bunraku and Kabuki, closely interrelated, were mere vulgar blood-and-thunder affairs by comparison with the aristocratic Noh drama always thought eminently suitable for samurai eyes.

When lord Asano was required to commit *seppuku*, this was not all: his domain was confiscated and given to another daimyo. His retainers were now without lord or employment. They became ronin. One of Asano's chief retainers, Ōishi Kuranosuke, summoned them all to a gathering and asked how many would be ready to join him in plotting and securing the death of the Lord Kira, the Bakufu official on whose account their own daimyo had gone to his death. Kira, an exceedingly avaricious and conceited man, had been offended when Asano, whom he had to instruct on certain points of shogunal court etiquette, had offered him what was evidently an inadequate gift. Accordingly Kira had been grossly insulting to Asano, the provocation being such that the latter

The story of the forty-seven ronin is the most famous vendetta in samurai history. These men undertook their revenge on Lord Kira knowing full well that it would cost them their lives. Above: The tombs of the loyal band stand in a row at the Sengaku-ji Temple. They have been the object of popular veneration ever since the incident.
Right: Also in the grounds of the Sengaku-ji Temple is this well at which Ōishi Kuranosuke, the leader of the ronin, washed Kira's head before placing it in front of the tomb of his dead lord, Asano

drew his dirk in Yedo Castle and attacked Kira, thereby sealing his own fate and that of his domain.

Only 46 of the Akō samurai, now ronin, responded to Ōishi's appeal and joined him. How many, in an earlier, or later, age would have volunteered can only be guessed. It is sufficient to say that the ronin of Akō knew they were dead men from the moment they made their resolve.

Extraordinary care was taken to throw Kira, their enemy in Yedo, off his guard. Ōishi took to a life of dissipation in the pleasure quarters of Kyoto, going so far as to divorce his wife to whom he had been married for 20 years. So well did he play his part that he would often be found asleep in a drunken stupor in the street. One day a Satsuma samurai recognised Ōishi in this condition and trod on his face and spat at him to show his disgust at such behaviour.

When they judged that Kira no longer feared revenge, the ronin—who now numbered 46 in all—attacked his home in Yedo, in accordance with tactics planned and directed by Ōishi. They sent messages at the same time to the houses of the neighbourhood explaining the purpose of their action. It was a snowy night in deep winter: a scene to be engraved sooner or later on the imagination of nearly everyone in the land.

Kira was found concealed in a closet. Ōishi courteously invited him, in language adjusted to Kira's high rank, to perform *seppuku*. 'I myself' Ōishi assured him, 'shall have the honour to act as your second, and when, with all humility, I shall have received your lordship's head, it is my intention to lay it as an offering upon the grave of Asano Takumi no Kami'.[18] But when it was seen that the invitation was rejected, Kira was killed with the dirk that Asano had used for his own *seppuku* more than a year before. Kira's head was then taken to Asano's tomb at the Sengaku-ji Temple in the Takanawa quarter on the other side of Yedo. As Ōishi and his followers made their way there they received many expressions of admiration from both samurai and townsmen. Having delivered their enemy's head at the temple they surrendered to the city magistrates.

A keen and in many ways recondite debate ensued as to what punishment, if any, should be awarded the loyal band. Meanwhile the ronin, treated as honoured guests rather than prisoners, awaited in the homes of various daimyo the decision of the Bakufu. The various schools of Confucianism and all the pundits of *bushidō* agreed that the action of the ronin had been inspired by the highest motive. Confucius himself had said a man could not live under the same heaven as his father's murderer and in the thinking of the samurai one's lord was more than a father. Powerful voices spoke up in favour of clemency, including, it is said, Tsunayoshi himself. But the act of vendetta, though sanctioned morally, was forbidden in Yedo and certain other cities. After about two months, sterner views having prevailed, the ronin were given the sentence they expected. Following their *seppuku* their tombs joined that of their lord, Asano, in the Sengaku-ji. As they have done ever since, people flocked to burn incense before the headstones. Among the first pilgrims was the samurai from Satsuma who had abused the drunken Ōishi in Kyoto. He bowed in apology before Ōishi's tomb and committed *seppuku*. His tomb was placed beside that of the 46 ronin.

Within a matter of a few days a Kabuki play about the vendetta was being performed in Yedo. It was almost immediately banned, but before long playwrights got round the difficulty by setting the story in an earlier historical period. As with the saga of Yoshitsune and Benkei, many embellishments were added to the tale which was circulated among the people not only by word of mouth, but also in puppet drama and Kabuki play, and in numberless publications. It did not escape the notice of contemporaries that Ōishi had been profoundly influenced by the teachings of Yamaga Sokō, exiled in the Akō domain. Thus, at the very moment when, as some thought, it showed signs of flagging, the samurai spirit had been dramatically revived.

SAMURAI IN SOCIETY

Women, love and loyalty

'Approach your husband as you would Heaven itself: for it is certain that if you offend him Heaven's punishment will be yours.' This admonition comes from the famous work known as the *Onna Daigaku,* to be translated literally as *Great Learning for Women* but best rendered perhaps as *The Whole Duty of Woman.* This may have been the work of the scholar, Kaibara Ekken (1630–1714). An innovator of some importance—he was the founder of medicinal botany in Japan—Kaibara was a wavering, critical, adherent of the neo-Confucian school. He enjoyed a very happy, though childless, marriage that lasted for 45 years. It is thought nowadays that it was his wife rather than Kaibara Ekken himself who was the author of the *Onna Daigaku.* In view of the harshly anti-feminine flavour of the work this may seem surprising, but it seems certain that in Tokugawa Japan, especially among the samurai class, the female sex no less than the male accepted the Confucian principle of the *sanjū,* the 'threefold submission' required of a wife: submission to her husband's parents, to her husband, and to her adult male offspring.

The *Onna Daigaku* has been described by a modern Western scholar as 'a *Bushidō* for women'.[1] The demands it made on the fortitude of young wives will be apparent from the following quotations:

> 'A woman has no particular lord. She must look to her husband as her lord and must serve him with all worship and

Left : Tales of Ise *from a sixteenth-century screen by Mitsuyoshi. Ancient tales of romantic love were curiosities in strict samurai society*

reverence, not despising or thinking lightly of him. The great life-long duty of a woman is obedience. In her dealings with her husband both the expression of her countenance and the style of her address should be courteous, humble, and conciliatory, never peevish and intractable, never rude and arrogant —that should be a woman's first and chiefest care . . .

'A woman must ever be on the alert and must keep a strict watch over her own conduct. In the morning she must rise early, and at night go late to rest . . .

'As a woman rears up posterity, not to her own parents, but to her father-in-law and mother-in-law, she must value the latter even more than the former and tend them with all filial piety. Her visits, also, to [her] paternal house should be rare after marriage . . .

'However many servants she may have in her employ it is a woman's duty not to shirk the trouble of attending to everything herself. She must sew her father-in-law's and mother-in-law's garments and make ready their food. Ever attentive to the requirements of her husband, she must fold his clothes and dust his rug, rear his children, wash what is dirty, be constantly in the midst of her household, and never go abroad but of necessity . . .

'The five worst maladies that afflict the female mind are indocility, discontent, slander, jealousy, and silliness. Without any doubt these five maladies infest seven or eight out of every ten women, and it is from these that arise the inferiority of women to men. A woman should cure them by self-inspection and self-reproach . . .

'We are told that it was the custom of the ancients on the birth of a female child to let it lie on the floor for the space of three days. Even in this may be seen the likening of man to Heaven and of woman to Earth; and the custom should teach a woman how necessary it is for her in everything to yield to her husband the first, and to be herself content with the second, place . . .

'If a woman act thus, her conjugal relations cannot but be harmonious and lasting, and her household a scene of peace and concord.'[2]

Such injunctions formed part of the curriculum of the *terakoya,* or temple schools for the primary education of the common people. Thus, the heavy emphasis on the second-class status of women, particularly evident in the samurai order, was fairly typical throughout society. Only uneducated peasant women, it seems enjoyed a degree of freedom denied their betters.

It is worth pointing out that with the abolition of feudalism in the 1870s more enlightened opinions began to undermine the precepts and spirit of the *Onna Daigaku.* Moreover, it has to be remembered that if the role prescribed for the samurai wife implied both hardship and subservience, the life-style of her husband, if he lived up to its stringent demands, was no easier. The Spartan nature of those demands is indicated by the fact that the samurai, when still a boy, was usually warned by his father that the three human functions of ingestion, excretion, and copulation must always be performed as speedily as possible, any temptation to dwell on the pleasure of such acts being most sternly resisted.

Human psychology, it seems, includes the phenomenon of the passing on of oppression. So one cannot but suspect that the samurai, under the weight of the obligations and self-discipline imposed by his code, may have sought some relief by inflicting on his wife some of the pressures that bore down upon him. In the same way a wife could have her revenge

Bunraku puppet theatre became one of the most important forms of drama in Japan, mainly through the brilliant plays of Chikamatsu Monzaemon who wrote at the turn of the eighteenth century. The audiences were mainly composed of townspeople, but samurai would often defy the Bakufu's interdict and attend performances. Above: The head of a Bunraku puppet.
Right: A performance of Chikamatsu' famous play, Imoseyama Onna Taikir (Household Teachings for Women at Imo and Se Mountains). *The play is a tragedy resembling* Romeo and Juliet *and concerns the forlorn love of the son and daughter of two opposed aristocratic families*

when the time came for her to receive a daughter-in-law into the household. Dutiful young wives were notorious for becoming tyrannical mothers-in-law in later life.

The inferiority of the female sex was less loudly proclaimed before the Tokugawa age. While it had always been implicit in Confucian ethics, it was given a new force by the widespread propagation of neo-Confucian ideas in the seventeenth century; and this trend was enhanced by the peaceful conditions that obtained after the middle years of that century. In earlier and more unsettled times a warrior's wife was expected to be more than a cook and a mother. As the daughter of a samurai—few warriors married outside their class—she would be trained in the use of the halberd and in the care and exercise of her father's horse; and she would be taught how to kill herself, should need arise, by stabbing her jugular vein with a *kai-ken* (pocket poniard). Such skills were not wholly forgotten during the Tokugawa peace, but the need for them became much less apparent. Thus for the wife of the Tokugawa samurai her role as partner in the face of danger diminished, became indeed unnecessary. On the other hand, among farmers, artisans and merchants it was the common practice for the wife to help her husband in his daily work. In those classes, therefore, the marital relationship rested on a less unequal basis than that generally accepted in samurai society.

Marriage was seen by all classes as a social duty, as an undertaking in which individual preference must yield to the interests of the families

concerned. In the samurai class, above all, the factors of social duty and family interest were of paramount importance; and the higher the rank, the greater the element of calculated family interest. In the case of the daimyo and their chief counsellors, the system of alternate attendance in Yedo necessarily involved fairly prolonged separation between husband and wife. The conjugal ideal, it is true, implied that love would follow marriage, sooner or later; the exemplary self-sacrifice and obedience of the wife would draw a response from even the most despotic husband. That this often happened is certainly true, but open acknowledgement of the fact, except in muted terms, was thought to be somewhat indecent. To praise one's wife was to praise oneself, and was therefore a breach of good manners.

From the point of view of contemporary European society, the lot of the samurai woman could be considered bleak. In the history of the Western world the term, 'chivalry', although wholly equine in its etymology, acquired connotations of gallantry towards the opposite sex that find little or no echo in the life and thought of the typical samurai. In his tradition, after all, there never existed the joust, adjudged by a woman and fought in her honour or for her favour.

Does this mean, then, that in the 'Way of the Samurai' there was no place for romantic love between the sexes? Officially at least, and for most periods, it was a firm precept that the ideal samurai should not be involved in an affair with a woman. Samurai society was not the world of Genji. Indeed, until well into the Tokugawa period Murasaki Shikibu's novel was generally regarded as lewd and corrupting. By the eighteenth century, however, disapproval was less widespread; and there ensued a reassessment of *Genji Monogatari* which, beginning with the claim that despite its superficial eroticism the novel had been written to uphold moral principles, proceeded to judge the work by strictly aesthetic

Left : A group of elegant villas in Yokohama now thought to be from the palace of the daimyo of Kishū though often associated with Hideyoshi's fabled Jurakudai palace. It represents the typical structure of high-ranking samurai villas.
Above : The interior of a villa used by the wife of the feudal lord, with a biwa, or lute, against one wall

criteria. It was argued, for example, that just as lotus flowers bloom in muddy water, so from illicit love affairs could spring manifestations of delicate beauty and feeling. The very fact that such mature criticism attracted the interest, as it did, of educated people, most of them samurai, indicates a loosening of the severe, didactic atmosphere commonly associated with the Tokugawa ruling class.

Grim stoicism, when it avoids the downward path to brutality, is by no means incompatible with finer feelings, and may in itself nurture an exquisite, if undeclared, appreciation of the yearnings and attachments of the heart. *Ninjō*—human feelings—moved the samurai, we may be sure, as much as any other man. But for the samurai more than any other man, *ninjō* could not be allowed to weaken his obedience to the call of duty. For duty—*giri*—was always imperative, showing the only way in which obligations (*on*) could be in part repaid. *Giri* applied supremely, as we have seen, to the relationship between the samurai and his lord. Second to that came his relationship with his parents, which was pervaded by both *giri* and *on*.

In the nature of things there was often conflict between duty and feelings, between *giri* and *ninjō*, and in most cases it is safe to suppose that it was resolved in favour of *giri*, whatever heart-searchings were involved. But there were of course acute situations in which the outcome remained for some time uncertain or could only emerge in a tragic form. It is not surprising, then, that the clash of *giri* and *ninjō* was the stuff of much stage drama and fiction. For the values of *giri* and *ninjō* can be nicely balanced; they may be said to be complementary. More than this, they have, in the broadest sense, a universal application: 'Giri not softened by ninjō may seem inhuman: it denies the individual's right to be happy at the expense of society. Ninjō unchecked by giri, however, is not only self-indulgent but can in the end destroy human society.'[3]

Prudence alone might well incline a samurai to act with restraint in matters of *ninjō*. To be torn apart by the conflict of love and duty was an agony not lightly to be endured. This was understood well enough by samurai wives and mothers. Since *giri* should always prevail, it was best to make the struggle easier by giving *ninjō* as little sustenance as was compatible with domestic harmony. So within a wife's subservience and docility there was also the spirit of the Roman matron: *dura virum nutrix*; a hard nurse of men.

In the hierarchy of samurai relationships, however, *giri* was much more than is implied by the single word 'duty'. Duty has, after all, a somewhat cold, even bloodless, connotation. It was here that the factor of romance, often absent or muted in other relationships, was allowed to come into play. Nitobe speaks of 'the peculiar strength and tenderness of friendship between man and man, which often added to the bond of brotherhood a romantic attachment doubtless intensified by the separation of the sexes in youth—a separation which denied to affection the natural channel open to it in Western chivalry.' He goes on: 'I might fill pages with Japanese versions of the story of Damon and Pythias or Achilles and Patroclos, or tell in Bushido parlance of ties as sympathetic as those which bound David and Jonathan.'[4]

Much the same point is made by the well-known Japanese social anthropologist, Chie Nakane. She offers the penetrating observation that 'in Japan there is no love story comparable in popularity to the Forty-Seven Ronin', for the story illustrates 'in extreme form the ideal personal relationship (always in terms of superior-inferior) in Japanese eyes'.[5] She argues that men involved in this kind of relationship 'have little room left for a wife or a sweetheart'; the emotions of a samurai 'would be completely expended in his devotion to his master'. There would be, it appears, no necessity for a love affair with a woman. This may have been, Dr Nakane suggests, the real nature of the samurai mentality.

There is surely much truth in this. It raises of course the question of homosexuality, whether unconscious or conscious. Homosexual practices,

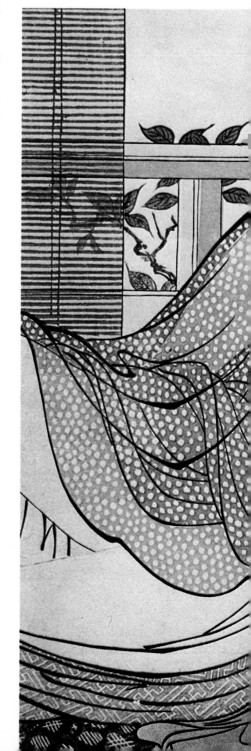

Below : Late eighteenth-century print or Ukiyo-e, *which means literally 'portrait of the floating world'. This is the work of the famous artist Utamaro and it is likely that the man portrayed is the artist himself, since he was a life-long devotee of the more elegant aspects of Yoshiwara life. Yoshiwara, the famous pleasure quarter of Yedo, was patronized mainly by the merchant class, but samurai – and ronin in particular – were not always reluctant to seek its varied delights*

o far as we know, were probably rife between Buddhist priests and their
colytes. There were many stories about homosexual love in these circles
during the Muromachi age (1339–1573), and in the sixteenth century the
European Jesuits and Franciscans in Japan noted with concern and dis-
pproval the prevalance of homosexual activities among their enemies,
he Buddhist priests. However, homosexual amours were not confined
o the temples. In at least one of his books, the seventeenth-century
writer, Ihara Saikaku, praised the love of men, rather than women,
among the samurai class. But he may have written in such terms in order
o ingratiate himself with the government of Tsunayoshi, 'The Dog
Shogun', who had a notorious fondness for young men. In any case,
hara Saikaku's considerable literary reputation has always rested on his
kill in depicting the life of merchants and other townsmen. Most of his
samurai heroes, it has been suggested, 'are drawn without any trace of
either criticism or humour' . . . It is not clear how much personal contact
Saikaku actually had with the samurai class. His townsmen have an
uthentic ring to their last detail, but his samurai tend to be schematized,

and their love affairs are almost invariably portrayed in terms of flawless devotion. Conceivably Saikaku's only object was to cater to samurai readers, but more likely he believed the samurai did in fact possess virtues beyond the attainment of the merchant class. The samurai lovers are depicted in Grecian terms as warriors who scorn the love of women but are ready to die to prove their unwavering love for another man. Again and again these stories end with the *seppuku* (ritual disembowelment) of both young men, each determined not to seem less than a hero in the eyes of the other.'[6]

Those comments by Professor Donald Keene include two points of particular relevance to a study of the samurai. There is the reference to the belief that samurai virtues were beyond the grasp of lesser mortals and there is the implied parallel with the practices of ancient Greece.

That a writer such as Saikaku, a master of irony and worldly humour, should have portrayed the samurai in idealized terms could mean that he was writing with his tongue in his cheek. But this would not necessarily signify lack of respect for those samurai who really did live up to their own demanding standards. Those standards, fully observed no doubt by only a minority of Japan's moral *élite*, nonetheless imposed respect. Nobody, however cynical, was likely to deny the righteousness of such standards, for they required a degree of dedicated self-sacrifice beyond the capacity of the average human being. Societies nurtured by the Christian tradition display a like contrast between ideals and reality. Only the truly insensitive in these societies have failed to accord some respect to those who have tried to shape their lives in accordance with the teachings of the Sermon on the Mount. For to love one's enemies and to tender the right cheek after the left cheek has been struck imposes an enormous strain on the psychic structure of natural man. 'We needs must love the highest when we see it': the context here may be Tennyson's Arthurian Court, but the words are equally applicable to feudal Japan.

The parallel with ancient Greece is suggestive, although it should not be overemphasized. *Seishinteki-ai*, 'spiritual love', can be faithfully

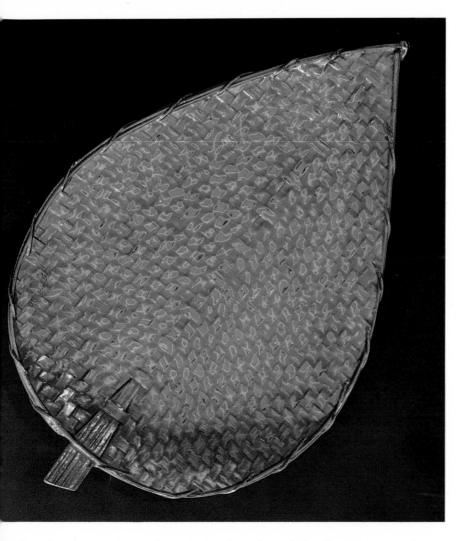

During the eighteenth and nineteenth centuries Japanese arts and crafts developed within the strict conservatism imposed by the Tokugawa Bakufu. Far left: A fan painted by a member of the Tosa school, portraying a court scene.
Left and below: Items used in the tea ceremony – which became somewhat vulgarized in the late Tokugawa period. The elegant tray is of lacquered bamboo; the cup bears the popular image of Fuji

endered as 'platonic love'; and the devotion of the Japanese warrior to his suzerain, which was demonstrated again and again as both precept and example, could be an emotion so consuming as to permit very little competition from the female sex. Habit illumined by affection no doubt bound the samurai to his spouse. Since sexual fidelity on the husband's part was not exalted as being in itself a particular virtue, dalliance with courtesans, provided it was light-hearted and unostentatious, was seen as no better and no worse than other forms of male amusement. Pleasure in itself, however, since it implied self-indulgence, was on the whole deprecated by the sterner arbiters of samurai ethics. As in the Greek city states, then, women in samurai society were valued as potential or actual mothers or were recognized as entertainers, the providers of fleeting physical joys. But to be distracted by the love of a woman—whoever she might be—was usually regarded at best as unseemly or unmanly, and at worst as a shameful disaster, the end of which was likely to be tragic, involving at least one, and probably two, suicides. To fall romantically in love with anyone or anything outside the charmed circle of one's superiors and peers would be to create a *giri-ninjō* crisis of unmanageable proportions.

Accordingly it is credible that many a samurai in his emotional life had 'little room left for a wife or a sweetheart'. It is also probable—although it is impossible to be dogmatic about this—that the samurai of all periods felt little need to connect *seishinteki-ai,* 'spiritual love', with physical sexual expression.

But how did matters stand in the vertical relationship between parent and son? Devotion to one's parents, we have seen, was recognized as more than a natural human instinct; it was a binding ethical imperative, being of course a manifestation of filial piety, which in the samurai scale of

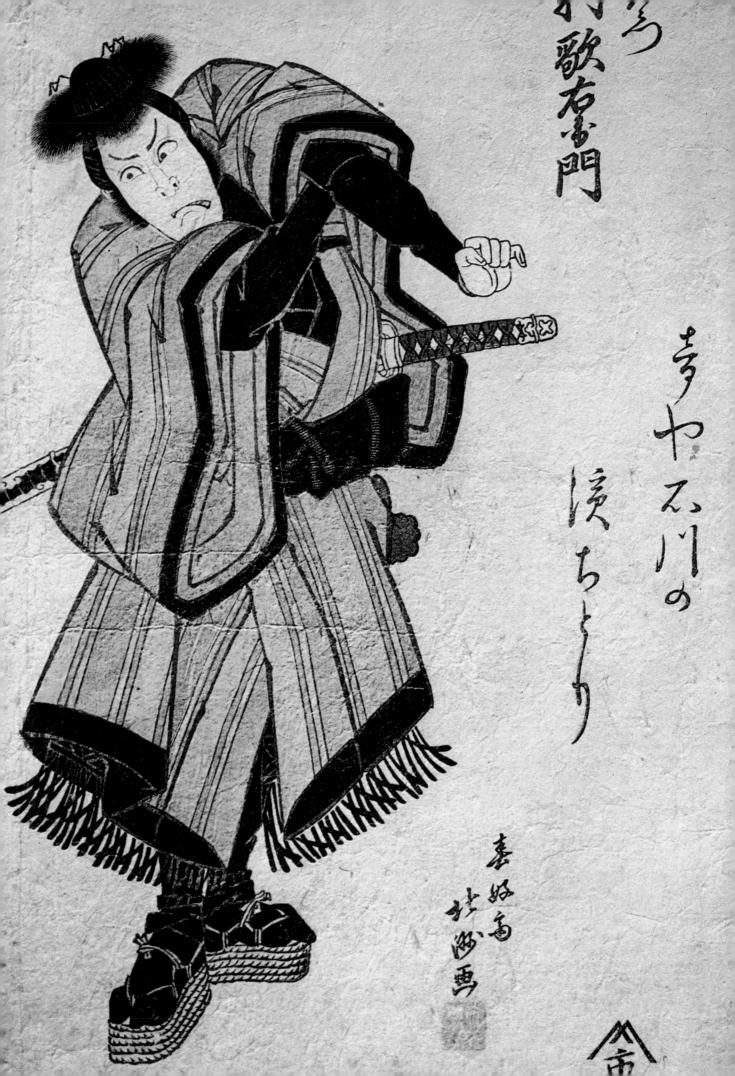

alues came second only to loyalty. It goes without saying that the obligations of son to father were expressed in terms of both love and obedience. As for the ties binding a son to his mother throughout his life, these do not appear to have been adversely affected by the convention that a mother ought to obey him after he reached manhood. It seems likely that any emotional starvation suffered by the wife in her relationship with her husband may have been alleviated by the intensity of the vertical ties between herself and her children. This would have applied to her sons in particular, since a daughter on marriage 'returned' to her bridegroom's home. Self-denial in the cause of caring for a widowed mother was as highly regarded in the samurai class as in any other section of society. Hideyoshi treated his aged mother with unremitting love and care, keeping in touch with her by letter when he could not be with her.

Indeed, this form of filial piety—that is to say, the care of a mother by a son—could even usurp the paramount position enjoyed by loyalty. The most famous example was provided by the scholar-samurai, Nakae Tōju (1608–48), often described as the founder of the Wang Yang-ming school in Japan. The Wang Yang-ming school of neo-Confucianism—known in Japanese as *Ōyōmei gaku*—cut across some of the lines of conduct so firmly drawn by Yamaga Sokō and the proponents of *bushidō*, for it emphasized the need to match words with action. What conscience dictates must be expressed in deeds; and conscience is the voice of the intuitive moral sense of the individual. Nakae's conscience prompted him to leave the service of his daimyo in order to return to his birthplace, there to look after his mother in her old age. He abandoned his function as a serving samurai without obtaining permission. The move cost him dear in terms of his livelihood, but it was generally recognized by critics and admirers alike as an unselfish act based on a definite, if unorthodox, philosophical and ethical point of view. It was not therefore a case of the *giri-ninjō* conflict, but rather of one kind of *giri* superseding another.

The relationship between father and son in samurai society was based, as in the Roman Republic, on love masked by severity. Respect fortified by fear seems to have been the dominant emotion of the warrior's son, who in emergencies might be charged when still a child with a weight of responsibility scarcely tolerable for one so young. A father's death could mean that a son became head of the family while still a boy. In the ages of civil war manhood came early, as one celebrated story of the fourteenth century serves to illustrate.

A famous warrior, Kusonoki Masashige, revered by posterity as the beau ideal of the loyal samurai, was accompanied on his way to what he knew to be a hopeless battle by his son, Masatsura, who is said to have been no more than ten years of age. Many historians now believe the boy to have been a good deal older, but as Ivan Morris puts it: 'In a study of Japanese heroism what matters is not the story's authenticity but its existence'.[7] Before reaching the battlefield his father told Masatsura to go home, to look after his mother. Kusonoki Masashige warned the boy that he might hear news of his father's death, in which case he was to go into the mountains and resist the enemy to the last. As the warrior had foreseen, the battle went against him; and he was heavily wounded before committing suicide by *seppuku*. This last act by Kusonoki Masashige was shared by his brother, who declared, just before he killed himself, that he would like to be reborn seven times in order to destroy their enemies. The brothers, having cut open their bellies, stabbed each other with their swords and died together.

In due course the enemy commander sent Kusonoki's head to his widow. The boy, Masatsura, retired to another room, bared his body and prepared to kill himself with a sword his father had given him as they parted before the battle. He was about to plunge the blade into his abdomen, when his mother discovered him and told him that it was his duty to remain alive.

A traditional saying in Japan has it that the three most alarming

Above : A beautifully painted screen with the recurring themes of sun and sea dating from the late seventeenth century.
Left : Samurai ethics were portrayed in the Kabuki theatre and in prints drawn from Kabuki such as this one from a series by Hirosada. The actor Nakamura Utaemon is shown in the role of Ichikawa Goemon, a samurai who tries to avenge the death of his father at the hands of Hideyoshi – called Hisayoshi in the play – by disguising himself as a high official. Vengeance for a father's death was an imperative for any samurai

phenomena in life are 'Fire, Earthquake, and Father'. Fear no doubt lost its edge after childhood, but some degree of awe remained. The obligation to a parent could never be fully repaid, and even death itself did not end the relationship. In front of the household *kami-dana* (family altar) reports would be made to a deceased father as if he were visibly, as well as spiritually, present in the room.

The fact that even this immensely powerful moral commitment of son to father should give way, according to the samurai code, to the greater obligation of the warrior to his lord shows very clearly the strength and quality of the ties that bound a samurai to his feudal superior. A classic exposition of the meaning of this kind of loyalty is the compilation known as the *Hagakure (Hidden Among Leaves)*, the work of a samurai of the Nabeshima fief in Kyushu during the early eighteenth century. The work breathes both poetry and narrow provincialism; for everything begins and ends with the Nabeshima fief. The *Hagakure* declares that since neither the Founder of Buddhism nor Confucius was ever employed by the Nabeshima House their teachings were not consonant with the traditions of the fief. In other words, the samurai serving the Nabeshima daimyo had need of no religion beyond their duty to their lord.

'Wherever we may be, deep in mountain recesses or buried under the ground, any time or anywhere, our duty is to guard the interest of our Lord. This is the duty of every Nabeshima man. This is the backbone of our faith, unchanging and eternally true.

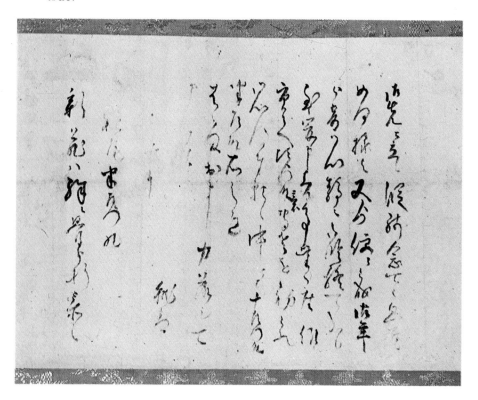

Above: Matsuo Bashō, (1644–1694), revered as the greatest of Haiku poets, was born a samurai but lived the life of a monk. In this message, written just two days before his death, he apologises to his disciples for dying before them. Death pervaded his poetry (see the first page of this book). Right: A lone monument standing in the grounds of the Kinkaku-ji, Kyoto

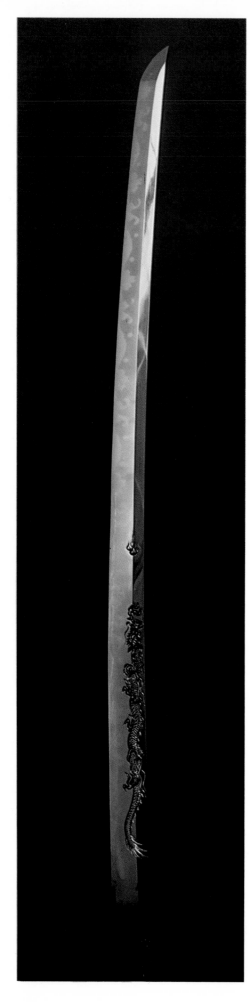

'Never in my life have I placed mine own thoughts above those of my Lord and master. Nor will I do otherwise in all the days of my life. Even when I die I will return to life seven times to guard my Lord's house . . .

'Every morning make up thy mind how to die. Every evening freshen thy mind in the thought of death . . .

'Bushidō, the way of the warrior, means death.'[8]

We should note that loyalty and filial piety had become a single ethical entity in which the duty to one's father was superseded by the duty to one's lord. This was a good way of forestalling any clash between these two supreme moral imperatives. For example, it was generally accepted that if a samurai opposed his lord, it was a son's duty to support the lord even against his own father. By a curious logic, the son's behaviour could then be considered 'filial piety at its highest'.

The *Hagakure* seems to advocate blind loyalty *per se*. But in fact—whatever may have been the case in the Nabeshima fief—the samurai had not only the right but also the duty to protest whenever he was convinced that his lord's action was foolish or unjust. Remonstrance, if all persuasion failed, must either be abandoned or take the form of suicide. That ultimate step was a very powerful sanction, enough to shake the determination of all but the most hardened and obstinate of feudal masters. Failure to remonstrate, in firm but respectful tones when occasion arose, could be viewed as disloyalty as well as moral cowardice.

The ideal samurai, while ready at any moment to sacrifice his life in the cause of loyalty, was no unthinking fanatic. For all the weight of external obligations that pressed upon him he was not relieved of a duty owed to his own conscience. This was particularly true in the case of those who embraced *Ōyōmei gaku*, the Wang Yang-ming school of learning, with its stress on intuition and on the importance of the unity of belief and action. Here a considerable impetus was given to the instinct for thinking things out for oneself; which could lead of course to a certain genuine independence of mind, as when Natae Tōju decided to look after his mother. This was one good reason why the Tokugawa government tended to regard *Ōyōmei gaku* with suspicion. Sincere belief in any faith, however unorthodox at first sight, could appeal strongly to the samurai mind. Evidence of this is provided by the conversion of so many Kyushu warriors to Christianity, and by the scarcely believable courage with which some of them faced a martyr's death. Thus, in practice it was not possible for the Bakufu to confine the samurai class strictly within any kind of ideological straitjacket, although an impressive measure of outward conformity was undoubtedly maintained.

However, a remarkable breach of the peace took place at Osaka in 1837. This was a rising by hungry citizens led by a prominent samurai scholar and former magistrate, Ōshio Heihachirō. Drawn to *Ōyōmei gaku,* he had made a pilgrimage to the birthplace and final home of Nakae Tōju on the shore of Lake Biwa. Crossing the lake on the way back, his boat ran into a storm, and it seemed likely that he would be drowned. As he contemplated the prospect of imminent death, Ōshio had a vision of being directly confronted by the Chinese sage, Wang Yang-ming, himself. 'This mystical experience on the lake', writes Ivan Morris, 'may well have propelled Ōshio to total emotional commitment and prepared him for his final action and death in a way that no amount of study or abstract reasoning would have achieved'.[9]

The 'final action', for which Ōshio has always been remembered, was his armed insurrection against the Bakufu authorities. This was inspired by his sympathy with the economic distress of the common people of Osaka. Through a combination of bad harvests and official mismanagement the city had been hit by a famine, and the poor faced starvation. Having failed by remonstrance to move the seemingly callous heart of the chief government official, Ōshio sold his large library of scholarly

Arms and armour underwent some changes in the relatively peaceful Tokugawa period, but always referred back to the times when they had been used in earnest.
Left: A masterpiece of the later swordsmith's art, this blade has been delicately engraved with a dragon motif.
Above: A tsuba, or sword-guard beautifully decorated with engravings of an eagle grasping a monkey in its talons. It is made of iron and the engraving is done in brass, the use of hard metals demonstrating that the piece is not only decorative but also serviceable.
Right: Fine armour made in the mid-eighteenth century for a member of the Matsudaira family. Like most armour of the period it borrows many of its features from previous eras, but unlike earlier armours it has been 'tested'. This refers to the fact that both the cuirass and helmet bear small pockmarks from matchlock balls which were fired at the armour from 30 paces to prove its strength

books in order to raise money for the poor, and also to purchase secretly a supply of arms.

The revolt, when it erupted, was only momentarily successful. Following its suppression Ōshio was eventually hunted down by the Bakufu. His end came in the flames of a house deep in the countryside, when in the face of his enemies he killed himself while the building crackled and crashed around him.

What is of interest is not so much the tragic revolt itself as the fact that it was planned and led by a samurai. Moreover, he was no mere rootless ronin but a respected scholar and former official. It is noteworthy that Ōshio's banners in the revolt bore the legend: 'Save the People!' It is as though the English Peasants' Revolt had been headed not by Wat Tyler and John Ball but by one of the king's own barons.

That at least is one way of looking at Ōshio's rebellion, and many a modern Japanese scholar has seen it in that light. But others, more prudently and perhaps more correctly, argue that the Osaka insurrection of 1837 can scarcely be interpreted as a truly revolutionary event. There does not seem to have been a widespread intention to turn the existing structure of society upside down. The object of the rising, so far as Ōshio was concerned, was primarily to register a fierce protest against intolerable conditions, and to punish hard-hearted officials and greedy rice-brokers. Ōshio himself displayed an independence of mind, and an active humanitarian spirit, that have given his name a lustre as yet undimmed. It is of some interest, perhaps, that during his career as an official he uncovered and destroyed a nest of secret Christians; and one is rather tempted to interpret the vision on Lake Biwa as a kind of Pauline conversion. Be that as it may, at a conscious level Ōshio was driven by the force of *Ōyōmei gaku,* the uncompromising character of which is well demonstrated by his heroic, if hopeless, revolt.

A truly revolutionary movement of the samurai or any other class in feudal Japan, although conceivable, would be extremely unlikely since it would have had to embrace as one of its aims the abolition of the imperial house; otherwise it would fall short of genuine revolution in the fullest sense. Shinto and the line of emperors being so intertwined as to be virtually synonymous, total revolution, in default of an injection of new faiths from abroad, could only imply spiritual collapse and nihilism.

While it is true that during most of the Tokugawa age, as well as in earlier periods, most samurai concentrated their thoughts on their duty to their immediate lord, so that Kyoto did not greatly impinge on their minds, this does not mean that they had no awareness of a national identity. They cannot have failed to appreciate that, if the shogun exercised the actual powers of central government, supreme spiritual authority was vested from ages past in the person of the reigning emperor. Distant and powerless as he might be, the emperor radiated a light of which all but the most doltish were aware. Putting it at its lowest, the emperor was taken for granted, like the sun. Nobody toyed with the ridiculous idea that he could be extinguished.

Nothing approaching this high status was to be enjoyed by the Tokugawa ruling house, even if Ieyasu's successors, by deifying him at his great mausoleum at Nikko, hoped otherwise. Of course, as one shogun succeeded another, with ritual proceedings such as 'alternate attendance' establishing, generation after generation, a rhythm of their own, the Bakufu acquired a seemingly permanent and impregnable solidity. Peasant risings and other signs of unrest there might be, but these were readily suppressed before serious trouble arose. The intelligence system of the Bakufu was elaborate and well maintained; little could escape its surveillance.

Yet it is one thing to control men's actions, quite another to ensure that their thoughts do not stray beyond officially approved limits, although it must be said that the Yedo government went some way towards achieving that goal. There arose, however, an indirect challenge, which

Below : While the Tokugawa shogunate endured as the centre of power in Japan, the growth of Kokugaku, or national studies, led to a resurgence of feeling for the imperial house and the role of the emperor. Even at Nikko, centre of the greatest of monuments to the Bakufu, this bridge, known as the 'Sacred Bridge', was designed for use only by the emperor or his special envoy

proved very difficult to deal with. From around the middle of the eighteenth century, intellectual circles—and the good samurai was always encouraged to cultivate his mind no less than his moral character and martial competence—became increasingly fascinated by what was called *Kokugaku,* or 'national studies'. This had two sides to it, one sustaining the other. *Kokugaku* meant in essence the reading and appreciation of early Japanese mythology, history, and poetry. From this sprang new emotional attachments both to Shinto and to the imperial house.

A development of this kind could not be blatantly opposed by the Tokugawa Bakufu. Japan had always been the Land of the Gods. Japan had always been reigned over by a single line of divinely descended emperors. The consequence of an enhanced awareness of these unique

The samurai helmet had always been used as a showpiece to make the warrior recognizable on the battlefield. During the peaceful Tokugawa era helmets began to take on even the most impractical and fanciful styles.
Above: A graceful design in the form of a shell, dating from the Momoyama period and finished in red lacquer.
Right: A far more extreme example dating from the early Tokugawa period. The grotesque dolphin has been built up in leather and lacquered red and black. With its eyes of gilded copper and its gold lacquered fins it presents a fearsome sight

national attributes was the spread of patriotic sentiment among the educated sections of the population. This was not something that any government could in logic deplore or afford to discourage. On the other hand, the greater the attention given to the imperial house and to its history the less importance, in the long run, might be attached to the position of the Bakufu. The study of ancient history was bound to make clear that there had been a time when Japanese emperors actually ruled as well as reigned.

In rather more recent periods, moreover, there had been occasions when for a short time the imperial house had managed to regain political power. This had occurred, for example, in the fourteenth century, between the collapse of the Kamakura regime and the beginning of the Ashikaga shogunate in Muromachi. Indeed, Kusonoki Masashige's great reputation for loyalty, which was later to become the centre of a cult arose from his devotion to the Emperor Go-Daigo, who had contrived to win back for a time the governing powers of the throne.

It was a process that had germinated for many decades, but by the early years of the nineteenth century a good many samurai, thanks to *Kokugaku,* were beginning to question the legitimacy of the Tokugawa government. Was it right that it should monopolize all the administrative functions which in ancient days pertained to the imperial house? Was there a case for suggesting that the Bakufu had usurped powers that should belong to the throne? Would the country be better governed from Kyoto?

These were dangerous thoughts indeed. To utter them openly was to invite arrest. But they provided an ideological rationalization for grievances against the Bakufu, and they were nursed in the heart. Over the years they eroded in a subtle, indefinable way the prestige of the government in Yedo, until the process culminated in the Meiji Restoration of 1868.

No doubt this erosion might have continued for a very long time without bringing about the collapse of the Bakufu, had not external events intervened in the nineteenth century to hasten the process set in motion by the spreading influence of *Kokugaku* ideas. It was the menace of foreign intrusion that put the Bakufu to the test. For the shogun's authority, his essential claim to legitimacy, depended in the last resort on his imperial commission as 'Barbarian Suppressing Generalissimo'. What would happen to his authority if it was clearly shown that he was unable to suppress the barbarians?

The small group of Dutch merchants that constituted the sole European settlement on Japanese soil had never presented any problem to the authorities. For the Dutch traders were confined to Deshima island in Nagasaki Bay and were normally permitted only brief and limited access to Nagasaki itself. Those few Hollanders, and some Chinese and Koreans, were the only foreigners allowed to set foot in the country. Once a year the 'Hollander Captain', as the director of the trading post was called, was required to make the journey to Yedo, to pay his respects and deliver reports to the shogun. His progress to Yedo was a foreign version of a daimyo procession; although curiosity rather than genuine respect must have been the common attitude of those who watched his party go by. No foreigner, after all, could be a samurai. In any event, the Dutch were merchants who gave Japan a small window on the world and provided a few useful and interesting products, including some books, mostly Dutch, on scientific subjects. Not until the eighteenth century was there anything like an unrestricted importation of books from overseas; and then any favourable reference to Christian teaching was enough to condemn a publication in the eyes of the Bakufu. In any event, there were few who were competent to read the foreign, mainly Dutch, books that arrived in Nagasaki, although gradually there came into being a corps of specialists, students of *Rangaku,* or Dutch studies.

When, as happened at fairly rare intervals, ships of other countries put in at a Japanese harbour they were always told to go to Nagasaki if they

needed urgent supplies of food and water. Once at Nagasaki, these vessels were well surrounded by guard-boats and were pressed to complete their business as quickly as possible. No contact with ordinary people ashore was permitted. Bakufu officials felt a sense of relief when the unwelcome visitor weighed anchor and made for the open sea.

In the nineteenth century unauthorized arrivals of this kind increased. For one thing, the development of the American whaling industry brought more vessels to the North Pacific; and the vicissitudes of the

Below: A samurai residence in Iga Ueno surrounded by peaceful paddy-fields. This area was the centre of one of the two major schools of ninjutsu

whalers—storm damage, shortage of supplies, illness among the crew— made it necessary for some of them to call at Japanese ports. There was also much increased Russian activity in the areas of Sakhalin and the Kuriles. At the same time, as the century advanced, British interest in China led to war and the acquisition of Hong Kong. These indications of greater American, Russian and British activity did not pass unnoticed by the Bakufu, or indeed by many samurai in the provinces. News from abroad might be sketchy, but it was on the whole reliable. For example, the Dutch were able to give Yedo advance notice of the United States Navy's intention to visit the Ryukyu Islands and Japan. The Bakufu, therefore, was not taken wholly by surprise by the arrival of Perry's squadron of two steamers and two sailing ships in July 1853.

Commodore Perry seemed to be totally indifferent to the presence of 5,000 samurai at the ceremony in which he handed over to envoys of the Bakufu a letter from President Fillmore. This requested the opening of trade; and Perry declared that, short of an immediate and favourable answer, he would have to come back in the following spring to discover what the reply might be. He made the point that on the second visit he would be in command of a much larger force. Before departing from Japanese waters Perry took his squadron up Yedo Bay to within sight of the city suburbs.

One can say that in this crisis samurai feeling, dictated by upbringing and by every reflection on past history and traditions, must have been one of profound anger. If the Bakufu had issued a summons to the military class, and indeed to the populace as a whole, to prepare for war it would have been obeyed with enthusiasm. Some eight months, perhaps, would elapse before Perry's 'Black Ships' returned—time enough, given Japanese energy, for the mustering of armies and the preparation of defences. On the other hand, Perry was not the only intruder. Admiral Putyatin's Russian squadron had tried to exert pressure on the Bakufu by anchoring in Nagasaki Bay for three months from August 1853.

The fact that the Bakufu did not adopt the heroic, if logically foolish, course of resisting the foreigners was a serious blow to its prestige. The samurai class as a whole could no longer feel that Yedo was in control of events. The treaty signed with Perry on his second visit, and the treaties subsequently signed with other countries, were negotiated, as was clear to all, under duress. No such humiliation had been experienced, or even imagined, in the recorded history of the country.

The treaties with the foreigners, opening certain ports to trade, were seen as merely the first step, after which the intruders would sooner or later advance to the occupation of the country as a whole. It was well known that this process had already taken place in the Philippines and on the Indian sub-continent, and it seemed to be happening nearer home on the China coast. As one samurai wrote to a friend: 'If this country is taken over by the foreigners, there will be no use in living and no other way for my whole family than to die . . . Though Japan is a warriors' country, it is a small country . . .'[10]

In addition to the not unnatural anxiety about the ultimate intentions of the foreigners, the samurai class felt uneasiness on other grounds. They had seen that the reaction of the common people to both American and Russian sailors—from the squadrons of Perry and Putyatin—had been, in general, one of friendly curiosity. Ordinary folk did not seem to be aware of the grave political implications of these visitations, while the foreigners often showed such familiarity and goodwill towards the common people that educated men wondered whether the existing class hierarchy could withstand the strain. In short, the arrival of foreigners was not only a threat to national independence but was also subversive of public order. There was a danger that the samurai class would no longer be able to retain its long established moral and ethical ascendancy. Yet in the agonizing process of Japan's adjustment to the importunate modern world it was the samurai in a new guise who led the way and set the pace.

THE BLACK SHIPS

The samurai
meets the modern world

The nineteenth century is replete with instances of vigorous martial *élites*—Maori, Sikh, Sioux, and Zulu—falling before the superior fire power of the Western world. 'We have got the Gatling gun and they have not.' Therein lay the confidence which in the final analysis sustained what was generally known and accepted in the West as 'the advance of Civilization', supplying the moral and intellectual credentials of that phrase with a force that was irresistible. The successful resistance of the Amharic empire of Ethiopia to the Italian invasion of the 1890s was the only exception to what had become the general rule.

In the case of Japan there was no co-ordinated armed action to oppose the West. There were, however, clashes between the foreigners and two important fiefs, those of Chōshū (at the western end of the main island) and Satsuma (southern Kyushu). An international squadron had no difficulty in destroying Chōshū fortifications at Shimoneseki in 1863, but the foreign ships were not content with shelling the forts; landing parties overcame samurai resistance and were able to dismantle the shore batteries already damaged by the earlier bombardment. The Satsuma town of Kagoshima was shelled by the Royal Navy; but here the proceedings were less humiliating to samurai pride. There was no landing of bluejackets, and although Kagoshima was set ablaze by the fire from the ships, the ships, too, suffered some casualties and damage from Satsuma batteries. So when the British squadron sailed away, the Japanese warriors could console themselves with the thought that the British admiral had shown less valour than discretion.

Apart from these sharp, if fairly brief, skirmishes, the skill and courage of the samurai as a class were not put to the test of battle. It was left to individual warriors to demonstrate, in a few violent episodes, their chagrin at the unedifying condition to which their country had been reduced. Acts of savage protest were directed against two targets: the Bakufu itself, as being responsible for the national loss of face, and resident or visiting foreigners, the symbols of arrogant intrusion.

Considering the intensity of the feelings aroused, there were fewer such acts of protest than might have been expected. The most famous explosion against the Bakufu occurred one snowy day in 1860 outside the Sakurada-mon (Cherry-field Gate) of the shogun's castle at Yedo, when the chief minister of the regime was cut down by a group of samurai from the Mito fief, which was well known as a centre of the *Kokugaku* ('national studies') cult. The Bakufu had not only concluded treaties with the foreign powers against the declared wishes of the Kyoto court, but was also engaged in persecuting samurai dissent with extreme vigour. As for attacks on foreigners, these caused great alarm from time to time. The British Legation in Yedo was assailed at midnight by a posse of swords-men who had taken an oath to massacre its inhabitants. The attack was beaten off at the cost of some bloodshed. A paper was recovered from a dead body indicating the thoughts and aims of the attacking party. It read, in part: 'Though I am a person of low standing I have not the patience to stand by and see the sacred empire defiled by the foreigner . . . Though being altogether humble myself, I cannot make the might of the country to shine in foreign nations, yet with a little faith and a little warrior's power, I wish in my heart, though I am a person of low degree, to bestow upon my country one out of a great many benefits. If this thing from time to time may cause the foreigner to retire, and partly tranquillise both the minds of the Mikado and of the Government I shall take to myself the highest praise. Regardless of my own life, I am determined to set out.' [1]

In or near Yokohama there were several murders of foreigners, often seemingly haphazard and unprovoked, by warriors who were not only offended by the presence of these aliens, but were also no doubt anxious to embroil the Bakufu in war. Samurai swords can cut a body to pieces in minutes; and the dead presented a horrifying sight.

Two worlds were now face to face. That they achieved fairly soon an uneasy co-existence, interrupted by occasional bloody affrays, is, all things considered, somewhat surprising. One might have expected them to be locked in irreconcilable conflict from the start. But the samurai of the nineteenth century, faced with the problem of dealing with the foreigner, were not of one mind. Although almost all of them, in the early days at any rate, would have welcomed the permanent departure of the long-nosed, blue-eyed traders and diplomats living in their midst, there was sharp disagreement as to the best way of achieving this aim.

During the period 1853–1868, known as the *Bakumatsu*, or 'twilight of the Bakufu', there were broadly speaking three main schools of thought. There was the official line taken by the Yedo shogunate; namely a reluctant recognition of the inevitability of foreign intercourse, based on an appreciation of the overwhelming material superiority of the Great Powers. Then there were those who felt that Kyoto and Yedo should join forces, sharing the government. Advocates of this course were samurai of a reforming sort, still ready to respect and sustain the Toku-gawa Bakufu but charmed by the idea of an active imperial presence in the national administration. The third main body of opinion took as its slogan the phrase, *Sonnō-jōi* ('Revere the Emperor, Expel the Bar-barians'). At its crudest, this was xenophobia of a virulent kind. It was also associated with disgust at the tyranny and incompetence of the Yedo regime and its alleged cowardice towards the Powers. One can label these three schools of thought as conservative, moderately radical, and ex-tremely radical. And the three differing general views were to be found in one way or another throughout samurai society.

Thus, the arrival of the foreigners not only threw the samurai into bitter dispute as to how to deal with them, it also provoked what was virtually a national debate about the way the country should be governed. And, as we might expect, it was among the samurai class that this debate took its keenest as well as its most violent form. Pragmatism and ferocity, compromise and idealism were basic components in samurai attitudes.

The final outcome after 1868, following the fall of the Bakufu and the Meiji Restoration has always seemed quite astonishing. For it was the extreme party, which included the myrmidons howling for the foreigners to be expelled, that emerged victorious. And yet, from the ranks of these warriors came the prime architects of modernization, working in overt harmony with the so-called Barbarians themselves. Having achieved power, they promoted the totally unhistorical myth, encouraged by the early Meiji oligarchy, that the Bakufu in the 1860s had shown no interest in modernizing the country.

The hero of these patriotic and radical samurai, particularly of those who were young, was a man of genius from Hagi, the headquarters of the Chōshū fief in western Japan. This was Yoshida Shōin, whose short life (1830–59) was marked by great intellectual activity, and an immense influence which was to become amplified after his death. That this should have been so has puzzled at least one famous expert on Japanese affairs, for Sansom remarks: 'It is not easy for a foreign student to understand why he so strongly influenced the minds of his contemporaries and was so extravagantly praised by later generations. It is clear that there is something in his life which appeals to the emotions of his compatriots...'[2]

The Japanese attitude towards the Europeans during the Yedo period was a mixture of fascination and rejection. The conflict between the appeal of Western technology and the fear of Western thought – regarded as degenerate – was particularly acute. Below: This portion of a screen painted in the late Momoyama or early Yedo period demonstrates the artist's fascination with the physique and dress of the namban jin, *or 'barbarians from the south'. He has shown Jesuit priests as well as traders. Far left: A 'daimyo' clock dating from the seventeenth century. Based on Dutch models, these clocks became an established feature of rich samurai households and were among a number of deliberate imitations of Western technology*

A glance at Yoshida Shōin's life and thought, then, will certainly throw considerable light on the psychology of the younger samurai who passed—or in some cases refused to pass—from one age to another between 1868 and 1878, from the world of castle-town and domain to that of the centralized modern state.

Yoshida Shōin was born into a family which provided an hereditary line of teachers at a long-established school for young samurai at Hagi. What they taught were the military arts and ethics propounded in the seventeenth century by Yamaga Sokō, the founding father of *bushidō*. Yoshida Shōin himself succeeded to this post, at least in the formal sense, at the tender age of six. He was something of a prodigy, for he appears to have delivered lectures (prepared by an uncle) by the time he was ten; and he was accepted as a fully fledged teacher when he was still only eighteen. His precocious ability impressed the lord of the domain, who encouraged him to pay a visit to Kyushu in order to study at Hirado, where the greatest authority on the thought of Yamaga Sokō maintained a school. A leading samurai at Hirado who had a notable library took an interest in the young man and allowed him free access to the books. In two months at Hirado Yoshida is said to have read some 80 volumes, including works on European history and geography.

Europe was brought closer to Yoshida when he moved from Hirado to Nagasaki, where he spent about a month; while there, he visited Dutch and Chinese residences and was hospitably received aboard a Dutch vessel. He showed particular interest in what the Dutch could tell him, through their interpreters, about the latest European technology, especially in gunnery. After returning home he was required to join his domain lord's progress to Yedo. In Yedo, although two years were to pass before the first appearance of Perry and the 'Black Ships', the smell of foreign pressure was in the air; and it is significant that Yoshida spent some days inspecting the neighbouring coastline as part of a defence planning exercise. His main *sensei* (teacher) at Yedo was an open-minded scholar interested not only in the various schools of Confucian learning but also in Taoism and Buddhism. 'The Way of scholarship', he told his pupils, 'demands that we should take the good from many sources.'[3] This eclectic outlook, very characteristic of the Japanese in the years ahead, greatly appealed to Yoshida, who decided to seek 'the good' by undertaking a journey to the north of the country.

Yoshida went first to Mito, north-east of Yedo, a noted centre of the patriotic cult, since it was in this fief that successive daimyo had encouraged the compilation of a huge work, the *Dai Nihon Shi* (The Great History of Japan). This placed great emphasis on the unique qualities of the imperial house and on the supreme virtue of those, such as Kusunoki Masashige, who had sacrificed their lives in the loyal service of the Throne. There emerged a specifically 'Mito school' of scholar-samurai; it was this school which first publicized the concept of the *kokutai*, a term that can be baldly translated as 'national structure'. But the word has deeper connotations, since it refers to what might be called the inner essence, or spirit, of the nation. It is therefore a term of potent talismanic value. After the Meiji Restoration it was to acquire general currency, but in the 1850s the word was unknown to samurai scholars out of touch or out of sympathy with the Mito school.

> 'According to *kokutai* thought, Japan is a patriarchal state, in which everyone is related and the imperial house is the main or head family. The emperor is the supreme father, and loyalty to him, or patriotism, becomes the highest form of Filial Piety. Because of the command of Amaterasu, this structure is both sacred and eternal; compliance with its requirements is the obligation and deepest wish of every Japanese'.[4]

From Mito, Yoshida Shōin travelled north as far as the Tsugaru

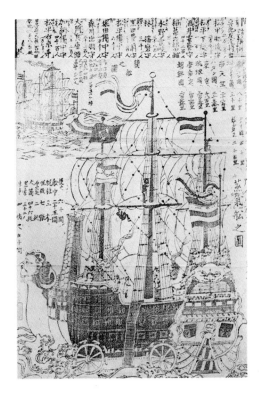

Above : A print by an unknown artist, probably dating from the 1850s, shows an attempt to meet the sudden need for understanding of the aggressive forces now encroaching on Japan. A somewhat naïve representation of an American steamship, obviously adapted from the artist's knowledge of sailing ships, is accompanied by details of its proportions and armament. Also listed are the distances to foreign countries – information that would have been little known during the years of isolation.
Left : Nationalist thought in any modern sense did not flourish until the major intrusions of the foreigners in the mid-nineteenth century. This print by Yoshitora, published in 1861, shows the influence in popular art of the new awareness of national identity

Right : Two suits of armour dating from the turn of the nineteenth century. The suits differ little in detail, but the smaller one was made for presentation during the ceremony of Gembuku. *This took place when a boy came of age, normally in his fourteenth year, and when his hair was dressed for the first time in the adult samurai manner.*

Far right : Tokugawa period scroll painting of the Ainu by an unknown artist, demonstrating a continuing popular interest in this barbarian people of northern Japan. When Yoshida Shōin visited them he found that 'the barbarians too are equally men'

straits, which separate Honshu from Yezo, as Hokkaido was then known. There he was both angered and saddened by the spectacle of the occasional foreign vessel (doubtless Russian) passing through the straits. In those remote parts he also came across some Ainu villages which had become Japanized. Yoshida was to write of the Ainu whom he encountered that there was no difference between them and ordinary people: 'so the barbarians too are equally men'.[5] This was far from being the general sentiment among the samurai class.

Yoshida's journey north had not been officially sanctioned by his daimyo. Accordingly, on returning to Yedo he reported at the Chōshū mansion in the city and requested punishment. He was told to go back at once to Hagi, to stay in his home there and regard himself as being under house arrest pending sentence. This was not to be delivered for some months. During this spell of enforced inactivity Yoshida read widely in the field of Japanese and Chinese history, and embarked on a further study of world geography and history. As his writings at the time reveal, he concluded from his studies that what had formed the character of 'The Imperial Land' (Japan) was its assertive foreign policy in ancient days. A return to a policy of expansion and conquest overseas became essential, since it would bring about the revival of Imperial Japan. In other words, a posture of defence was not enough. Japan must assert her power beyond her own borders. The war must be carried into the enemy's camp. Yoshida Shōin was not the first thinker of the Tokugawa age to advocate the abandonment of national exclusion in favour of a positive, expansionist foreign policy, but he was the most influential.

The domainal sentence on Yoshida, when it was finally announced, was a stiff one. He was dismissed from his lord's service and his name was removed from the samurai register. The daimyo retained a personal regard for Yoshida, however, and gave him permission to travel and study for the next ten years, whereupon Yoshida left for Yedo, and reached the city a week before Perry's squadron first arrived in Yedo Bay.

In Yedo, Yoshida met with a famous teacher, Sakuma Shōzan, a samurai who had added to his store of classical learning an impressive competence in Western military technology, acquired through the Dutch language. Sakuma's proficiency in mastering new fields of study is best illustrated by the fact that from instructions printed in Dutch texts he was able to build a camera and take a photograph of himself with it. He also published a Japanese-Dutch dictionary. His particular interest, however, was modern weaponry and he not only learned how to cast cannon but also became an expert in their use.

Yoshida had called on Sakuma, who was 20 years his senior, on his first visit to Yedo and had been enrolled as one of his many pupils. But it was only during his second visit that Yoshida, now a ronin, became closely associated with Sakuma. For with the arrival of the Black Ships he hastened to join Sakuma and a party of his disciples at Uraga, where they were watching with curiosity as well as indignation as the American vessels anchored off shore. Sakuma, needless to say, was doing his best to observe and record the shape and size of Perry's guns.

Sakuma Shōzan, Yoshida, and the others believed war was unavoidable, even though talks were in progress between Bakufu officials and Perry and his staff. However, Sakuma considered that whatever the outcome of the talks, talented young samurai ought to be sent abroad at once to investigate conditions in foreign countries and to purchase, with Dutch help, a number of modern, ocean-going, ships. Indeed, Sakuma formulated a principle that was to colour much of Japanese thought in the years ahead—a principle encapsulated in the slogan, 'Eastern morality, Western skills' This could not be put into practice, of course, unless the Bakufu was willing to lift the ban on foreign travel which had been imposed with the closing of the country in the first half of the seventeenth century.

Yoshida Shōin was ready to defy the ban by persuading a foreign vessel to take him on board as a passenger. This decision was reached, with Sakuma's blessing, after Perry's ships had departed. Accordingly, when news reached Yedo of the arrival in Nagasaki of Putyatin's Russian squadron, Yoshida set out for that city, the money for his expenses being provided by Sakuma Shōzan. Travelling by way of Kyoto (where he wrote a famous poem to commemorate his obeisance before the imperial palace) Yoshida reached Nagasaki only to discover that the Russians had sailed away four days earlier. He returned to Yedo, but he had been back in Yedo less than three weeks when Perry made his second appearance, with a more powerful squadron. Once again Yoshida and his friends believed war would surely come, and they discussed plans for the assassination of Commodore Perry. But when the Bakufu signed the Treaty of Kanagawa, it became clear that for a time peace would be maintained.

Yoshida now decided to take the hazardous step of trying to persuade the Americans to accept him as a passenger on one of their vessels. Perry's squadron had moved from Yedo Bay to Shimoda on the Izu peninsula, and there Yoshida contrived to board the American flagship during the hours of darkness. But Perry refused to connive at the violation of Japanese law that Yoshida's request would have involved.

This abortive venture was followed by the arrest of both Yoshida and Sakuma Shōzan. While in custody in Yedo, Yoshida (in a letter to his brother) justified his defiance of the ban on foreign travel by citing the example of the Forty-seven Ronin, who had broken the peace of Yedo in order to avenge their lord's death.

Transferred by the Yedo authorities to his own domain, Yoshida was committed to prison in Hagi, but was released after a year on condition that he lived with his family, his contacts being restricted to the family circle. This condition, however, was not enforced, and before long there gathered round Yoshida, in a school known as the *Shōka Sonjuku,* a small group—it never exceeded about 30 in all—of enthusiastic young disciples. They were taught military drill, gunnery and other technical subjects, but the main function of the school was to indoctrinate the young men with the *bushidō* ideals propounded by Yamaga Sokō and with a keen sense of loyalty to Emperor and nation.

Yoshida, being still only 27 years of age, was not much older than many of his pupils. They lived in close proximity with him—an experience, it seems, that nobody could forget. For in Yoshida Shōin was to be observed a remarkable combination of intellectual brilliance, unkempt appearance, and dishevelled attire, at first sight both droll and repulsive.

Yoshida in fact was now becoming a recognizable *shishi,* 'a man of

Below : Another print from the series by Hirosada. It shows a later scene from the Kabuki play about Ichikawa Goemon's attempt to avenge his father's death. In this scene he has succeeded in confronting the powerful Hisayoshi. The modern image of the samurai has been largely created by nineteenth-century popular art of this sort

spirit', or 'man of high purpose'. It was a term which was to come very much into vogue during the 1860s when Yoshida was already dead, and was used to denote those samurai, usually of humble rank, and frequently masterless ronin, who were ready to defy not only the Bakufu but also their own lord (if they had one) in the cause of Sonnō-jōi, 'Revere the Emperor, Expel the Barbarians'. The shishi lived dangerously, and their courage impressed posterity, giving rise to an extensive literature which was largely hagiographical in character. Sakuma Shōzan, Yoshida's mentor and benefactor, was to advocate the opening of the country to foreign intercourse so that Japan could become, as he put it, 'the leading nation of the world', and this ambitious dream inspired many shishi, for to see their nation as a world leader was one way of expelling the Barbarians. But this end could be achieved only under the banner of the Emperor and this new kind of nationalism—very much the product of the samurai spirit—brought the shishi into conflict with the Bakufu.

It was not only the Yedo government that harried 'the men of spirit', however. 'Opening the country', even in the glorious cause of advancing the power and prestige of Japan, was a slogan offensive to those die-hards who refused to have any truck with the foreigners. Thus, Sakuma Shōzan, who was imprisoned for some years by the Bakufu for his part in Yoshida's attempt to leave Japan, was assassinated by an anti-foreign fanatic.

Yoshida Shōin's pupils at Hagi formed a remarkable group; nearly every one of them was active in the movement that produced the Meiji Restoration or reached a high position in public life after the establishment of the Meiji government. Among them were two giant figures, who were later to dominate political life for several decades, Ito Hirobumi and Yamagata Aritomo. Yamagata's American biographer rightly emphasizes the influence exerted by Yoshida Shōin—whose first question to the young samurai was: 'Are you ready to die?'

One might say, indeed, that the Battle of Toba-Fushimi of 1868, in which the imperial forces led by Chōshū and Satsuma defeated the Tokugawa army—thereby reversing the verdict of Sekigahara—was won on the tatami of Yoshida's home at Hagi. For Yoshida came to accept the necessity of insurrection against the Bakufu, and he began to plot actively to this end, recruiting his own students as agents and fellow conspirators. Yet when he had made up his mind, Yoshida was never one for concealing his opinions; and the idea of throwing his opponents off their guard by deceit was totally abhorrent. Accordingly, he addressed a written memorial for the eyes of his daimyo, accusing the shogun of disloyalty to the imperial house. We have noted that Yoshida's suzerain, the lord of Chōshū, thought well of him, and criticism of the Yedo regime was by no means uncommon in his domain, so the open expression of Yoshida's subversive views incurred no penalty. It was another matter, however, when he tried to interest an official of the domain in a plan to assassinate a member of the shogun's council who had arrived in Kyoto and was intent on stamping out anti-Bakufu activities. Yoshida was immediately placed under arrest. After some six months of imprisonment he learned that orders had come for him to be sent to Yedo for trial. He was allowed to spend his last night in Hagi at home with his relatives. He reported back at the prison next day in the sure knowledge that sentence of death awaited him in Yedo. After a trial and a further period in custody at Yedo, the expected verdict was given. He was beheaded on 21 November, 1859, two months after his twenty-ninth birthday. A group of pupils, including Ito Hirobumi, took charge of his remains, Ito wrapping the body in his own juban, or undershirt.

Yoshida declared in his last will and testament that he would return to life 'seven times', to help in repelling the Barbarians. The reference to seven reincarnations is a conscious echo of the famous vow made at Kusonoki Masashige's seppuku. For among Yoshida's writings there is a tribute (Views on the Seven Rebirths) to Kusonoki, whom he greatly venerated. Kusonoki Masashige, it has been well said, 'represents an

Above: The legacy of the samurai. This helmet, green with mould, was recently discovered hidden away in the fourteenth-century home of a ronin family, the Hakogi.

Right: Half-mask, or hambō, *made in the eighteenth century by a member of the Myōchin family. The Myōchin were the leading armourers in Japan for more than 400 years of samurai history*

ideal vision of sincerity which, though it may illuminate the world for a while like a flash of lightning in a dark sky, is bound to be extinguished by impure reality.'[6] A similar claim can be made for Yoshida Shōin. Which explains why he could capture the imagination of the *shishi* and retain, in the later age of Japan's imperial expansion, an honoured place in the national pantheon.

It would be going too far to claim that before the Meiji Restoration Japanese patriotism was the monopoly of the samurai class; but because the samurai, in the estimation of others as well as themselves, were the supreme exemplars of the civic virtues, they were the leaders in thought and action during the transition from a feudal to a national society. Samurai dominated the new Meiji administration, even at the lowest levels. The police, in villages as well as towns, were for the most part former samurai. In industry, banking, and commerce a substantial proportion, probably a majority, of the new entrepreneurs were men who had exchanged a pleated skirt and two swords for trousers and a walking stick only a few years earlier.

In terms of a break with tradition, the metamorphosis of the warrior into a businessman was one of the more startling transformations wrought by the new age. Although there had always been cases of samurai joining the ranks of the merchant class, such instances were rare. For instance, Fukuzawa Yukichi tells us in his autobiography that his father, a samurai of relatively low rank, was horrified when he learned that his children were being taught arithmetic in the local domain school. He took them away, exclaiming that it was abominable that 'innocent children should be taught to use numbers—the instrument of merchants'.[7] The prejudice against samurai participation in trade and industry crumbled when it was explained (Fukuzawa's own writings and lectures were influential here) that such activity, 'for the sake of the nation', was perfectly honourable, and that the warrior could serve the Emperor as sincerely in the counting-house as on the parade ground.

So far as its traditional trappings were concerned—the hierarchy of Bakufu, daimyo, and retainers high and low—the Way of the Samurai disappeared. The apparatus of armour, winged helmet, banner and war-fan was put away, to be seen again only at one or two annual *jidai matsuri*, the 'period festivals' associated with certain shrines and localities. In this sense there was a clear break with the past. The division of society into the four main classes was abolished, and this alone would have been enough to put an end to the unchallenged hegemony of the warrior order. Furthermore, the carrying of two swords was first made optional and then forbidden. The rice stipends of the samurai were removed, the once-for-all monetary compensation being (except in the case of the daimyo) so ungenerous as to compel them to earn their own living.

These shattering assaults on the proud symbols and solid benefits of the warrior's status were planned and carried out by his own class. It was a curious revolution: the samurai had overthrown the samurai.

Yet at a deeper, less tangible, level the Way of the Samurai did not disappear. Rather it became in a diluted form the common property of a vastly greater constituency, colouring the ideas, feeding the emotions, and guiding the actions of millions who never had a sight of a two-sworded warrior, except perhaps on the Kabuki stage or, when the twentieth century arrived, in moving pictures. For the state educational system vigorously disseminated such essential concepts as loyalty, self-sacrifice, and a regard for the martial arts, thus preserving, sustaining and strengthening the ethics thought appropriate to an expanding Imperial Japan. Forty years after Yoshida Shōin's death, artisans, farmers, fishermen and shopkeepers could say to themselves: 'We are all samurai now'. The consequences, in terms of world history a few decades later, are well known. It required a second revolution, provoked like the first from outside, to give the restless ghosts of the samurai what may prove to be, perhaps, their final quietus.

CHRONOLOGY

The conventional division of Japanese history into 'periods' follows the names of the political capitals of the nation at that time, whether the capital was the residence of the emperor in pre-samurai times, or the residence of the shogun during the samurai era. There are alternative names for these periods, however, based on the first name, or family name, of the shogun. In this book both names have been used, and both are listed here.

Pre-samurai history begins in legend with the foundation of the empire by Jimmu Tennō in 660 BC. This chronology begins with the introduction of Buddhism into Japan during the sixth century AD.

Period Name	Date	Notable Events
	556	Introduction of Buddhism
NARA	710	Imperial capital established at Nara
HEIAN	794	Heiankyō (Kyoto) established as capital
	858	Establishment of Fujiwara regency
	935	Taira Masakado's insurrection in the east
	(Eleventh century)	Wars in the north; the emergence of the Taira and Minamoto as the leading warrior families
	1156	Hōgen Insurrection, Kyoto
	1159	Heiji Insurrection, Kyoto. Supremacy of the Taira under Kiyomori
	1170	The first recorded instance of *seppuku* (hara-kiri)
	1181	Death of Kiyomori
	1181–1185	The Gempei (Minamoto-Taira) War
	1184	Destruction of the Heike (Taira) at Dan-no-ura
KAMAKURA	1192	Minamoto Yoritomo becomes shogun; beginning of the Kamakura Bakufu
	1210–1333	Ascendancy of the Hōjō shikken (regents) at Kamakura
	1274	First Mongol invasion
	1281	Second Mongol invasion
	1333	Fall of the Hōjō and Kamakura
MUROMACHI (ASHIKAGA)	1336	Ashikaga Takauji becomes shogun, with his headquarters at Muromachi, Kyoto; the beginning of the Muromachi age
	1336–92	War between the northern and southern courts
	(Fifteenth century)	Intermittent civil war in many areas
	(Early sixteenth century)	*Sengoku-jidai*, 'The Age of the Country at War'
	1542	Arrival of the Portuguese; influx of Christian missionaries follows in the wake of Iberian traders
	1573	Oda Nobunaga deposes the last Ashikaga shogun
MOMOYAMA	1582	Death of Oda Nobunaga
	1582–98	Ascendancy of Toyotomi Hideyoshi
	1592	Hideyoshi's first invasion of Korea
	1597	The second invasion of Korea
	1598	Death of Hideyoshi
	1600	Battle of Sekigahara
YEDO (TOKUGAWA)	1603	Establishment of Tokugawa shogunate (Yedo Bakufu) at Yedo (Tokyo)
	1615	Battle of Osaka Castle
	1636	Sumptuary laws and regulations for the control of all classes; suppression of Christianity and closure of the country to all foreign intercourse, except for restricted trade through Chinese and Dutch merchants at Nagasaki
	1701–1702	The Affair of the Forty-seven Ronin
	1853	First appearance of Commodore Perry's 'Black Ships'
	1867–68	Fall of the Tokugawa shogunate; restoration of imperial power
	1869	Emperor Meiji moves from Kyoto to the new capital, Yedo, renamed Tokyo.

GLOSSARY

Ashikaga The warrior household which established its Bakufu in the Muromachi district of Kyoto in the fourteenth century.

Bakufu Literally, 'Camp Office': the name given to the shogun's government.

Bakumatsu The last years of the Tokugawa Bakufu, roughly from 1854 to 1867.

Bunraku The puppet drama, developed in Kyoto in the late sixteenth century; it flourished in Osaka, Kyoto, and Yedo in the Tokugawa era.

bushi A military man, a samurai.

bushi-no-nasaké A warrior's sense of mercy or benevolence, the Japanese counterpart of the European concept of chivalry.

Bushidō 'The Way of the Warrior'; the code developed very largely in the seventeenth century.

cha-no-yu The Tea Ceremony.

Chu Hsi Twelfth century exponent in China of the Confucian school of philosophy favoured by the Tokugawa Bakufu in the seventeenth century.

daimyō Literally, 'great name'; the provincial lord, at certain periods almost an independent monarch in his own territory.

Fudai The daimyo who actively supported Ieyasu at the battle of Sekigahara (1600). (See also *Tozama daimyō*)

Gempei The Minamoto and Taira warrior houses, whose struggle for power in the late twelfth century ended with the destruction of the Taira (Heike).

Genroku The era name for the years 1688 to 1704; associated with a hedonistic, extravagant phase of urban life.

giri Duty; obligation, notably to a superior (for example, one's lord or teacher); among the samurai *giri* took precedence over human sentiment. (See also *ninjō*)

hara-kiri Literally, 'belly cutting', the self-inflicted death held in honour by the samurai class. (See also *seppuku*)

Heian Derived from Heiankyō, an early name for Kyoto, and commonly associated with the culture that flourished in and around Kyoto from the end of the eighth century AD until the late twelfth century.

Kabuki Originating from a form of folk-dancing, Kabuki drama became popular during the late eighteenth century.

kaishaku-nin The assistant during the act of *hara-kiri* whose office was to strike off the head of the samurai who had been ordered, or had chosen, to commit self-immolation.

kami The deities of Japan.

Kamikaze 'The Divine Wind'—the great storm which destroyed the Mongol fleet in 1281.

karō Chief retainer of a daimyo.

Kokugaku 'National learning'; the study of Japan's ancient past, which acquired importance in the early nineteenth century.

kokutai A heavily emotional term, often translated as 'national polity'; refers to the unique characteristics of the Japanese national tradition.

Meiji The regnal name for the period 1867 to 1912. The Emperor Meiji presided over the modernization of Japan.

Minamoto The celebrated warrior family that defeated its rivals, the Taira (Heike), in the late twelfth century.

Momoyama The castle built by Hideyoshi near Kyoto. The name 'Momoyama' became associated with the art and fashion prevalent in the late sixteenth and early seventeenth centuries.

Muromachi The district in Kyoto in which the Ashikaga shogunate was established; the period 1339 to 1573 being generally known as the Muromachi age.

Nara Capital of Japan in the eighth century AD, noted for its Buddhist architecture.

ninja Name given to highly specialized spies, skilled in the arts of concealment, employed by contending warrior captains and daimyo, as well as by the Bakufu.

ninjō Human feeling; sympathy, kindness; these, according to the samurai code, must take second place when in conflict with the call of duty. (See also *giri*)

ninjutsu 'The art of invisibility', attributed to the *ninja*.

Noh Theatrical form of considerable antiquity, notably developed during the fourteenth century.

Ōyōmei gaku The school of Confucian thought named after the Chinese thinker, Wang Yang-ming (1472–1529); followers of this school emphasized independence of mind and the 'unity of thought and action'.

rōnin Literally, 'wave men'; samurai without a recognized lord; unemployed warriors, many of whom disturbed the peace of Yedo during the Tokugawa age.

sankin kōtai 'The system of alternate attendance', whereby every daimyo was compelled to spend a regular period in attendance at the shogun's court in Yedo.

sengoku daimyō The territorial lords prominent in the sixteenth century, when the country was in the throes of civil war (*sengoku* means 'the country at war').

seppuku The polite term for hara-kiri.

Shintō 'The Way of the Gods'; the indigenous faith of the Japanese, predating the introduction of Buddhism.

shishi 'Patriot'; the name given to those samurai who, in the years after Commodore Perry's arrival in 1853, were active in promoting the cause of an imperial restoration.

shogun 'Great general'; the title given to Minamoto Yoritomo and various successors. (See also *Bakufu*)

Shōka Sonjuku The small school at Hagi run by Yoshida Shōin, whose pupils included several future leaders of the nation.

Sonnō jōi 'Revere the Emperor: Expel the Barbarians'—the rallying cry of most *shishi*, implying not only the expulsion of foreign diplomats and traders but also the overthrow of the Tokugawa Bakufu.

Taira The warrior family that acquired control of the court in the twelfth century.

tatami The tight straw matting that fits together to cover the entire floor of a traditional Japanese room.

Tennō The Emperor.

tokkōtai Special attack corps; usual term for the suicide units of the Pacific War.

Tokugawa The warrior house descended from the Minamoto, which, under Ieyasu, established the shogunate at Yedo (modern Tokyo) at the beginning of the seventeenth century.

torii The gateway to be found at the entrance to a Shinto shrine.

Tozama daimyō 'Outside lords'—those who fought against Ieyasu at Sekigahara in 1600 or were otherwise hostile.

Wang Yang-ming See *Ōyōmei gaku*.

Yedo The old name for Tokyo.

Yoshiwara The main pleasure quarter of Yedo.

NOTES

Chapter One:
1 Varley *The Samurai*, 42
2 Kenzo *Ise, Prototypes of Japanese Architecture*, 14
3 Sansom *A History of Japan 1615–1867*, 237
4 Cooper *They Came to Japan*, 60–61

Chapter Two:
1 *Genji Monogatari* (The Tale of Genji)
2 Morris *The World of the Shining Prince*, 177
3 Sansom *A History of Japan to 1334*, 237
4 *Ibid.* 252
5 Shinoda *The Founding of the Kamakura Shogunate*, 49
6 Morris *The Nobility of Failure*, 367
7 Mishima *Sun and Steel*, 63
8 Mitford *Tales of Old Japan*, 235–236
9 Morris *The Nobility of Failure*, 67

Chapter Three:
1 Okakura *The Book of Tea*, 36
2 Suzuki *Zen and Japanese Culture*, 62
3 Herbert *Shinto*, 77
4 *Ibid.* 44
5 Suzuki *Zen and Japanese Culture*, 92
6 *Ibid.* 92
7 *Ibid.* 111
8 Sitwell *The Bridge of the Brocade Sash*, 117
9 *Transactions & Proceedings of the Japan Society, London*
   —Vol XI 1912–13, 146
10 *Ibid.* 153
11 Sansom *Japan, A Short Cultural History*, 397
12 Cooper *Southern Barbarians: The First Europeans in Japan*, 119
13 *Ibid.* 122
14 Tanaka *The Tea Ceremony*, 76–77, reprinted by
   permission of Kodansha International
15 Paine *The Art and Architecture of Japan*, 58
16 Tsunoda *Sources of the Japanese Tradition*, 329

Chapter Four:
1 Sadler *The Maker of Modern Japan: The Life of
   Tokugawa Ieyasu*, 214
2 *Ibid.* 277
3 Brinkley *A History of the Japanese People*, 570

4 Hall *Government and Local Power in Japan 500–1700*,
   345–346
5 Tsukahira *Feudal Control in Tokugawa Japan*, 76
6 Asakawa *The Documents of Iriki*, 336
7 Sadler *The Maker of Modern Japan: The Life of
   Tokugawa Ieyasu*, 390
8 Hyoe *Guides to Japanese Culture*, 159–160
9 Wright *Confucian Personalities*, 8
10 Satow *A Diplomat in Japan*, 37
11 Maruyama *Studies in the Intellectual History of
   Tokugawa Japan*, 124
12 Hall & Jansen *Studies in the Institutional History of
   Early Modern Japan*, 322–323, reprinted by
   permission of Princeton University Press
13 Maruyama *Studies in the Intellectual History of
   Tokugawa Japan*, 123
14 Reischauer *East Asia: The Great Tradition*, 309
15 Maruyama *Studies in the Intellectual History of
   Tokugawa Japan*, 328
16 Tsunoda *Sources of the Japanese Tradition*, 399–400
17 *Ibid.* 404–405
18 Mitford *Tales of Old Japan*, 24

Chapter Five:
1 Bellah *Tokugawa Religion*, 97
2 trans. of *Onna Daigaku* in Chamberlain *Things Japanes*
3 Keene *World Within Walls*, 260–261
4 Nitobe *The Soul of Japan*, 144
5 Nakane *Japanese Society*, 71
6 Keene *World Within Walls*, 190
7 Morris *The Nobility of Failure*, 385
8 Bellah *Tokugawa Religion*, 81–82
9 Morris *The Nobility of Failure*, 191
10 Livingston *The Japan Reader*—Vol 1, 85–86

Chapter Six:
1 Alcock *The Capital of the Tycoon*—Vol 2, 160
2 Sansom *The Western World and Japan*, 284
3 Earl *Emperor and Nation in Japan*, 115
4 *Ibid.* 237
5 *Ibid.* 118
6 Morris *The Nobility of Failure*, 289–390
7 Fukuzawa Yukichi *(Autobiography)*, 3

BIBLIOGRAPHY

ALCOCK, Sir Rutherford *The Capital of the Tycoon*—
2 vols (Longman Green, London 1863; Greenwood
Press, Westport, Conn. 1968)

ASAKAWA, K. (Ed) *The Documents of Iriki* (Yale University Press, New Haven 1929)

BELLAH, Robert N. *Tokugawa Religion* (The Free Press,
New York 1969)

BLACK, John R. *Young Japan, Yokohama and Yedo
1858–1879*—2 vols (Oxford University Press, Tokyo
1968)

BOLITHO, Harold *Treasures Among Men: The Fudai
Daimyo in Tokugawa Japan* (Yale University Press, New
Haven 1974)

BOWDEN, Sir Frank *The Japanese Sword in Legend, Story
and Fact* (The Japan Society Bulletin, Vol IV, No 6,
London 1969)

BRINKLEY, F. *A History of the Japanese People* (Encyclopedia Britannica, New York 1915)

CHAMBERLAIN, Basil Hall *Things Japanese* (J. Murray,
London 1905)

COOPER, Michael (Ed) *They Came to Japan: An Anthology of European Reports on Japan 1543–1640* (Thames & Hudson, London 1965; University of California Press, Berkeley, CA., 1965)

COOPER, Michael (Ed) *Southern Barbarians: The First Europeans in Japan* (Kodansha International, Tokyo 1971)

DUNN, C. J. *Everyday Life in Tokugawa Japan* (Tuttle, Tokyo 1972)

EARL, David M. *Emperor and Nation in Japan: Political Thinkers of the Tokugawa Period* (University of Washington Press, Seattle 1964)

FREDERIC, Louis *Daily Life in Japan at the Time of the Samurai*—trans. Eileen Lowe (Allen & Unwin, London 1972)

FREDERIC, Louis *Japan—Art and Civilization* (Thames & Hudson, London 1971; Harry N. Abrams Inc., New York 1971)

FUJISAWA, Chikao *Zen and Shinto* (Philosophical Library, New York 1959)

FUKUZAWA, Yukichi *(Autobiography)*—trans. D. E. Kiyooka (Hokuseido Press, Tokyo 1960)

GARBUTT, M. *Japanese Armour from the Inside* (Transactions & Proceedings of the Japan Society, Vol XI, 1912–1913, London 1913)

GRAHAM, Dom Aelfred *Zen Catholicism* (Collins, London 1964; Harcourt Brace Jovanovich, New York 1964)

HACKETT, Roger F. *Yamagata Aritomo in the Rise of Modern Japan* (Harvard University Press, Cambridge, Mass. 1971)

HALL, John W. *Government and Local Power in Japan 500–1700* (Princeton University Press, Princeton, New Jersey 1966)

HALL, John W. & Jansen, Marius (Eds) *Studies in the Institutional History of Early Modern Japan* (Princeton University Press, Princeton, New Jersey 1968)

HALL, John W. & Toyoda, Takeshi (Eds) *Japan in the Muromachi Age* (University of California Press, Berkeley, Calif. 1977)

HERBERT, Jean *Shinto* (Allen & Unwin, London 1967; Stein & Day, New York 1967)

HERRIGEL, E. *Zen in the Art of Archery* (Routledge & Kegan Paul, London 1953)

KEENE, Donald *World Within Walls: Japanese Literature of the Pre-Modern Era 1600–1867* (Secker & Warburg, London 1976; Holt, Rinehart & Winston, New York 1976)

KENZO, T. & Noburo, K. *Ise, Prototypes of Japanese Architecture* (M.I.T. Press, Cambridge, Mass. 1965)

LEWIS, Archibald *Knights and Samurai: Feudalism in Northern France and Japan* (Temple Smith, London 1974; Harper & Row, New York 1974)

LIVINGSTON, J. et al. *The Japan Reader*—2 vols (Pantheon, New York 1974)

McCULLOUGH, Helen *The Taiheiki* (Columbia University Press, New York 1959)

McCULLOUGH, Helen *Yoshitsune* (Stanford University Press, Stanford, CA., 1966)

MASS, J. P. *Warrior Government in Early Medieval Japan* (Yale University Press, New Haven 1974)

MARUYAMA, M. & Hane, M. *Studies in the Intellectual History of Tokugawa Japan* (University of Tokyo Press, Tokyo 1974; Princeton University Press, Princeton, New Jersey 1974)

MISHIMA, Yukio *Sun and Steel*—trans B. Bester (Secker & Warburg, London 1971; Knopf, New York 1971)

MITFORD, A. B. *Tales of Old Japan*—2 vols (Macmillan, London 1871)

MORRIS, Ivan *The World of the Shining Prince* (Oxford University Press, London 1964; Knopf, New York 1964)

MORRIS, Ivan *The Nobility of Failure* (Secker & Warburg, London 1975; Holt, Rinehart & Winston, New York 1975)

MURAKAMI, H. & Seidensticker, E. (Eds) *Guides to Japanese Culture* (Japan Culture Institute, Tokyo 1971)

NAKANE, Chie *Japanese Society* (Weidenfeld & Nicolson, London 1970; University of California Press, Berkeley, CA. 1970)

NITOBE, Inazō *Bushidō, The Soul of Japan* (Teibi, Tokyo 1920)

OKAKURA, Kakuzo *The Book of Tea* (Tuttle, Tokyo 1956)

PAINE, R. T. & Soper, A. *The Art and Architecture of Japan* (Penguin Books, Harmondsworth, Middx., 1955)

REISCHAUER, E. & Fairbank, J. *East Asia: The Great Tradition* (Houghton Mifflin, Boston, Mass. 1962; Allen & Unwin, London 1961)

SADLER, A. L. *The Maker of Modern Japan: The Life of Tokugawa Ieyasu* (Allen & Unwin, London 1937; AMS Press Inc., New York 1976)

SANSOM, G. B. *Japan, A Short Cultural History* (Appleton-Century, New York 1943)

SANSOM, G. B. *The Western World and Japan* (Cresset Press, London 1950; Knopf, New York 1950)

SANSOM, G. B. *A History of Japan to 1334* (Cresset Press, London 1958; Stanford University Press, Stanford, CA., 1958)

SANSOM, G. B. *A History of Japan 1334–1615* (Cresset Press, London 1961; Stanford University Press, Stanford, CA., 1961)

SANSOM, G. B. *A History of Japan 1615–1867* (Cresset Press, London 1964; Stanford University Press, Stanford, CA., 1963)

SATOW, Sir Ernest *A Diplomat in Japan* (Seeley Service, London 1921; AMS Press Inc., New York 1921)

SEWARD, Jack *Hara-Kiri: Japanese Ritual Suicide* (Tuttle, Tokyo 1968)

SHINODA, Minoru *The Founding of the Kamakura Shogunate* (Columbia University Press, New York 1960)

SITWELL, S. *Bridge of the Brocade Sash* (Weidenfeld & Nicolson, London 1959)

STORRY, Richard (Ed) *Mirror, Sword and Jewel* (Croom Helm, London 1973)

SUZUKI, D. T. *Zen and Japanese Culture* (Routledge & Kegan Paul, London 1959; Princeton University Press, Princeton, New Jersey 1959)

TANAKA, Sen'o *The Tea Ceremony* (Kodansha International, Tokyo 1973)

TSUKAHIRA, T. G. *Feudal Control in Tokugawa Japan* (Harvard University Press, Cambridge, Mass., 1966)

TSUNODA, R. et al. *Sources of the Japanese Tradition* (Columbia University Press, New York 1958)

TURNBULL, S. R. *The Samurai: A Military History* (Osprey, London 1977; Macmillan, New York 1977)

VARLEY, H. P. *The Ōnin War* (Columbia University Press, New York 1967)

VARLEY, H. P. et al. *The Samurai* (Weidenfeld & Nicolson, London 1970; Dell, New York 1970)

WARNER, L. *The Enduring Art of Japan* (Grove Press, New York 1952)

WRIGHT, A. & Twitchett, D. *Confucian Personalities* (Stanford University Press, Stanford, CA., 1962)

INDEX

ACKNOWLEDGMENTS

Werner Forman and the publishers would like to acknowledge the help of the following in permitting the photography shown on the pages listed:
Victoria and Albert Museum 6, 17, 22–23, 38 (top), 48, 49, 50–51, 94–95, 102, 103 (top), 121; Ono Collection, Osaka 8; Freer Gallery, The Smithsonian Institute 12; National Museum (Sato-ji), Kyoto 13; Nishi Hongan-ji, Kyoto 16, 29, 39, 57; Boston Museum of Fine Art 18–19, 24, 25, 27; Museum of Folk Art, Tokyo 20–21; Kita-In, Saitama 20 (top), 48 (top), 50; L. J. Anderson Collection 28, 36, 37, 51, 59, 80 (left and right), 81, 103, 106, 107, 116; Osaka-jo Tenshu-kaku, Osaka 38 (left), 90; To-ji, Kyoto 44; Imperial Household Agency 52, 53; Kongo Nogakudo, Kyoto 54, 55 (top); Seikado Library 55 (bottom); Art Institute of Chicago 58, 84–85, 113; Osaka-jo Tenshu-kaku (Kuroda collection) 65, 66, 67; Ninja Museum, Ueno 68 (left), 68–69; Myoju-ji, Kanazawa 74; Burke Collection 76–77; Mibu-dera, Kyoto 79; Dallas Museum of Fine Arts 88; Bunraku Kyokai, Osaka 91; Rinshun-kaku, Yokohama 92–93; Philip Goldman, London 97 (right); Collection of the late Joe Hloucha, Prague 98, 118–9; Basho Kenshokai, Ueno 100; Mr and Mrs C. D. Wertheim 110, 114, 115; Tempus Antiques Ltd. 112.

Werner Forman would also like to thank the following for their assistance:
Isamu Hakogi; Masaya Hirai; Hodo Oshita; Mr and Mrs Kiyoshi Ikeda; Kazuhiko Inada; Tadashi Inoue; Mikio Kato; Taro Kurabayashi; Tomikazu Nakade; Hiroshi Nakamura; Mr Okida; Mrs Haruko Sato and Michiko Sato; Riemon Sato; Ryozen Shioiri. With special thanks to: L. J. Anderson; Shigeyoshi Araki; Joe Earle; Zuiko Harita; Takami Ikoma; Shunkai Matsuura; Yosaku Tsushiya; The To-ji, Kyoto; The Jodo Shinshu Hongan-ji-ha, Kyoto; The Mibudera, Kyoto; The Kongo Nogakudo, Kyoto.